LEARNING TO SEE THE WORLD THROUGH

Drawing

LEARNING TO SEE THE WORLD THROUGH

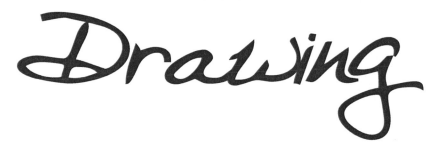

PRACTICAL ADVICE FOR THE CLASSROOM
Grades One through Eight

Elizabeth Auer, MEd

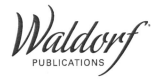

Printed with support from the Waldorf Curriculum Fund

Published by:
Waldorf Publications at the
Research Institute for Waldorf Education
38 Main Street
Chatham, NY 12037

Title: *Learning to See the World through Drawing*
   Practical Advice for the Classroom, Grades One through Eight

Author/Illustrator: Elizabeth Auer
Illustrations from the class of 2011, Pine Hill Waldorf School
"Reflections" illustrations: Thomas Buchanan, Elise Drapeau, Lily Hobbs, Emil Schroettnig,
   Steven Upton
Copy editor and proofreader for the author: Amy Hilbert
Copy editor and proofreader for Waldorf Publications: Melissa Merkling
Cover art: Elise Drapeau
Design and layout: Ann Erwin

Contents

Introduction

*"What the teacher can do is to point out the road that leads to
accomplishment and try to persuade her students to take that road.
This cannot be a matter of mere formula."*

– Kimon Nicolaïdes

This manual is a culmination of over twenty years
of teaching classroom drawing to students in the
Waldorf Teacher Training program at Antioch
University in Keene, New Hampshire, and teaching
drawing in the classroom in grades one through eight.

A background

Beginning as a student in Waldorf schools in the
Netherlands and in Great Britain, I have always had
a passion and interest for drawing.

After graduating from college with a Diploma in
Graphic Design, I worked in design studios in London
and Edinburgh, doing mostly illustration. Eventually
I found my way to New Hampshire where I discovered
desktop publishing and illustrating on the computer.
Gradually I developed a style of black and white
illustration with pen and ink and scratch-board, as
well as drawing with colored pencils.

Observing teachers

I have observed teachers in the elementary
grades for many years, in a variety of classrooms
and in different schools. I have watched them draw
with their students and have seen how the children
illustrated their books. Observing teachers' styles and
approaches has provided a great resource for ideas for
drawings, such as the calendar project for grade two
(see "The calendar").

Experience in the classroom

In drawing with children, nothing equals direct
personal experience in the classroom on a daily
basis from grade one through grade eight. I had the

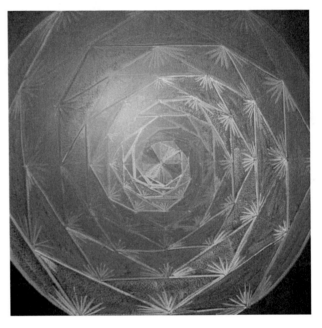

privilege of being able to observe the development of
children's drawing on a yearly basis and to see how
personal styles develop and can be recognized.

Starting in first grade allowed me to establish
expectations and classroom drawing etiquette that
created the foundation for very fruitful and enjoyable
years of artistic experience in the classroom, for both
the students and the teacher.

Workshops and courses

Offering workshops to parents broadened the
foundation, as I began to have additional experiences
while drawing with adults. Doing workshops in
drawing, painting and clay modeling for the Center
for Anthroposophy Foundation Studies Program
became an ongoing enlightening experience.

It was also during the first years of working as the Manual Arts Teacher at the Pine Hill Waldorf School that I was first approached about giving private drawing lessons to students training to become teachers. Mentoring of teachers in various schools on an individual basis has also been a significant part of the experience.

Master's thesis

Undertaking research on children's drawings for a Master's thesis offered an opportunity to further understand the significance and complexity of this activity. Having assigned the "Person, House, Tree" drawing exercise at the beginning, middle and end of each grade provided a rich archive of drawings done at different age levels.

Which road to take?

There are many roads that can be taken in a classroom, many different ways and formulas that can be tried and practiced. The work in the classroom is carefully prepared for the children that enter its door. How art is introduced and practiced varies greatly in different educational settings.

Rudolf Steiner education

In the Waldorf/Steiner schools, teachers follow a form of curriculum based on the foundations and guidelines of Rudolf Steiner's pedagogy. Art plays a very important role all the way through high school. Teachers who teach in Waldorf/Steiner schools have the enormous task of practicing many forms of art that are integrated into the curriculum. Drawing is just one of them.

Development of the drawing course

Drawing has been an important part of the Waldorf teacher education training course at Antioch New England Graduate School in Keene, New Hampshire, for most of its 21-year history. While it is a required course for the Waldorf education student teachers, students from other programs are also welcome to join the course and take what they learn to other school settings.

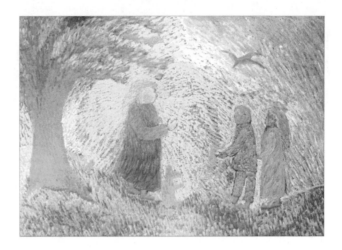

Course contents

The course includes crayon and pencil drawing as well as the art of blackboard drawing, with the main emphasis being on drawing to complement the main lesson books. The course has been taught in different formats and has evolved over time. It has been very beneficial and many non-Waldorf teachers have taken their experiences into various public and other private schools.

Approaches to drawing

Several approaches are described in this book, including an introduction to diagonal-shaded drawing and drawing with a breathing tone. Emphasis is placed on sculptural, three-dimensional drawing rather than linear drawing.

Art can be experienced by anyone in any school, and by adults in any educational setting. For instance, working with the block crayons with a more sophisticated veiling method can be much enjoyed by adults looking for stimulating artistic activity. It is also a very freeing experience for adults when they discover, with a small amount of guidance, that working with this medium creates lovely drawings, no matter what the level of artistic ability.

This book is primarily for

- The new teacher, who will be practicing drawing as part of her lessons in a Waldorf school and has not taken a course in classroom drawing.

- The experienced teacher who has not drawn since her elementary education and/or is new to teaching drawing as part of her lessons.
- A teacher in any public or independent school who may become intrigued to take up drawing with her students and integrate it into her lesson plans.
- Home-schooling parents who wish to follow the Waldorf curriculum and encourage their children to draw in their books.
- Any parents or teachers who wish to draw with their children.

The aim of this book is to cover all the basic questions and concerns that arise when drawing is taken up as an activity with children from ages seven through fourteen. It is intended as an aid for teachers by giving ideas for drawing to be made into large format in preparation for the lessons. The material covers the various approaches to drawing with children and addresses important issues such as drawing phobias that get in the way of success in drawing for both the student and the teacher.

Accumulation of notes and tips

Over the years the notes and tips, questions and answers have accumulated and have eventually found themselves bound together in this book.

In addition to serving the most basic needs of the new teacher and giving helpful tips and ideas for experienced teachers, there are also some much-needed tips for the left-handed teacher. The aim is to help the left-handed teacher orientate herself in a classroom where the majority of children will be right-dominant. As the subject of dominance is not the main focus of this book, left-handedness will be discussed in a general way for the benefit of both the student's and the teacher's drawing activities.

The essence

The chapters summarize the essence of the drawing experience in the elementary Waldorf/Steiner educational setting. The art of drawing described can be used in any other educational setting, regardless of its philosophy. Readers and future drawing teachers are invited to discover, see and determine for themselves what is appropriate for young children and their stages of development.

Think about how children can achieve sculptural drawing in three dimensions and at what stage this process should begin. Contemplate texture and the aesthetics of color. Wonder at edges of objects, what they are and how they mysteriously appear and disappear, depending on the point of view from which the object is observed.

Moving through the grades

I invite the reader to ponder what media and approach to use at what stage of the child's development and what the child is experiencing. The ultimate question surely is: Is what the child is experiencing conducive to integrated, whole learning? Is the drawing experience fostering a sense of self-confidence and enjoyment? Will the future adult have good memories of drawing in the elementary years, which will become the foundation for her subsequent drawing and enjoyment of the arts?

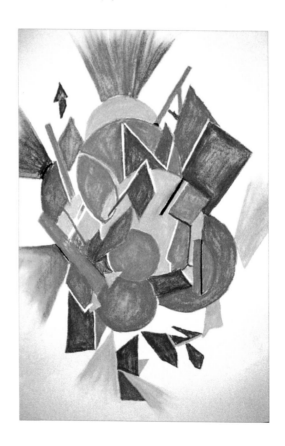

Classroom research

This chapter focuses on the development of children's drawings and how the teacher can benefit from observing how and what children draw at different age levels. It is based on direct classroom experience over eight years. This is followed by a study on the gesture and movement of children as shown in their self-portraits.

Education research – promoting reflective practice

The material on daily drawing in the lives of our children adds another perspective from a former colleague who is pursuing doctoral studies in educational leadership. Drawing promotes an inner habit of reflecting on what has been learned and on what pictures arise from daily lessons. This inner habit of reflection is discussed more fully in the chapter beginning on p. 115.

Reflections from students

Throughout the text of this book are comments from students who graduated grade 8 from Pine Hill Waldorf School in 2011. The book ends with a chapter devoted to their reflections during their sophomore and senior years in high school. A survey went out to students who had been with the class for most of the eight lower grades years. Their answers to the questions in the survey give full meaning to the significance of the teacher's guidance in their journey through the elementary years.

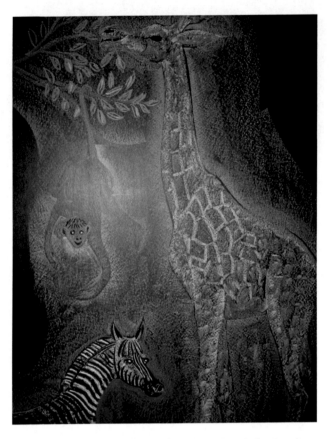

It is hoped that those of you who read this book will take what is given here as food for thought and action in the classroom; work with it in practice, observation and thinking, and, out of experience, follow what your own inner voice tells you. The important thing is that you come to understand what you are doing, why you are doing it and what benefits are finding their way to the children in the classrooms as they travel along their path of learning.

Do not think that you can learn drawing, any more than a new language, without some hard labor. But do not, on the other hand, if you are ready and willing to pay this price, fear that you may be unable to get on for want of special talent.
It is indeed true that the persons who have peculiar talent for art draw instinctively and get on almost without teaching. It is also true that it will take one person much longer than another to attain the same results, and the results are never quite so satisfactory as those got with greater ease when the faculties are naturally adapted to the study.
But I have never yet met with a person who could not learn to draw at all; and, in general, there is satisfactory and available power in everyone to learn drawing if he wishes.

– John Ruskin

What is drawing?

I do not yet know the actual character of the land at present.
I am drawing everything I come across now, and then later, when I have experience,
I will try to render it in its most basic characteristics.

\- Vincent Van Gogh

We all walk around in the world and see the landscape spread before us, but we often dream into what our eyes are beholding and don't really see what we are looking at. Putting pencil to paper and recreating what it is that we see helps us to understand what it is we are looking at. Drawing to recreate or to create what we see goes back a long way in human history.

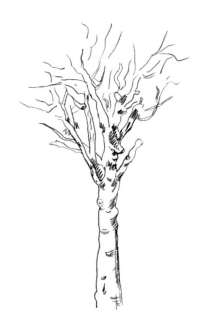

Looking back

From the very beginning of human evolution, we have been engraving images onto surfaces. Some of the earliest cave paintings were created with paints blown onto walls. Images were carved in relief with tools, and sculpture and painting were the main art forms. Tracing the outline of shadows of figures cast onto a wall by the light of a fire, candle or lamp played an important part in the development of drawing.

Drawing itself as a two-dimensional art form does not appear in the evolution of art until the time of the Greek vases, where within the contours of the black figures details were drawn in lines incised by a metal tool. Engraved bronzes dating back to the Etruscan

period (c.490 BC) are purely linear and come the closest to two-dimensional art. Engraving in copper was well known to the Italians in the 15th century and shows techniques of a combination of contours and parallel hatching to produce a distinct three-dimensional effect of light and dark.

The Renaissance

During the Renaissance in Italy, France and northern Europe, drawing was established as the basis of every genre of art and came truly into its own. There were many draftsmen of this time, the most well known among them Leonardo da Vinci (1452-1519), Michelangelo Buonarroti (1475-1564) and Raphael Sanzio (1483-1520). Drawings were done in a variety of different media, including pencil, ink,

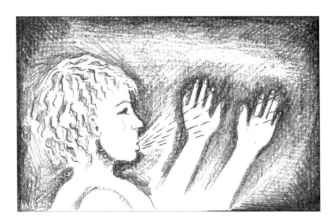

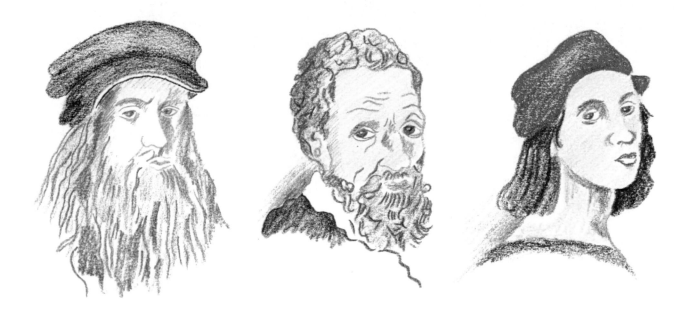

watercolor and ink washes of different colors, and chalk, and on a variety of different paper.

Drawings were often made as studies for paintings to follow, and many artists executed carefully detailed, finished studies for their paintings. The drawings served as blueprints for the workshop assistants who would transfer them onto the canvas or wall in preparation for painting.

In myriad drawings, Leonardo analyzed the structure of rocks, the behavior of light, the movement of water, the growth of plants, the flight of birds and the anatomy of insects, horses and human beings. His sketches were not only preparation for paintings, but also served to quench his thirst for knowledge and understanding of the world around him. Leonardo was a man ahead of his time; his visionary understanding gave us many glimpses of what the future would bring, such as the airplane.

Michelangelo used drawing as a medium for developing new ideas and conveying artistic thoughts. He also viewed his drawings as material needed for his work and used them, for instance, in his monumental task of painting the Sistine Chapel in the Vatican. Drawing was the basis for all his remarkable creative work.

Raphael explored and mastered the variety of drawing media and techniques practiced in his time, executing a vast number of studies. He would often combine drawings in pen and ink with washes in ink or lead white, applied with a brush in order to add tonal qualities. He also used red and black chalk. Drawings had a crucial function in the realization of Raphael's art and were the patterns for his final works.

Albrecht Dürer (1471-1528) developed the art of etching to the highest degree. Using curved and straight hatching and stippling, he created sculptural forms and physical beauty, as well as menacing shadows in dark forests.

Nicolas Poussin (1594-1665) was a leading painter in the Baroque style, following the High Renaissance. He was a prodigious draftsman, yet his drawings are unfinished and unpolished. He drew many variations of compositions repeatedly as preparation for his paintings.

Rembrandt van Rijn (1606-1669) was one of the greatest draftsmen in all of art history. He used his drawings for study and observation and brought spirituality to his etchings by rendering radiant light with a warm glow in many of his compositions.

Jean-Honoré Fragonard (1732-1806) was among the greatest draftsmen of the 18th century. He often used red chalk in his studies, and while Poussin did not save many of his drawings, as they were only meant as aids to his paintings, Fragonard often exhibited his drawings as well as his paintings.

Vincent van Gogh (1853-1890) began his artistic work as a draftsman, not as a painter, and produced over 1100 drawings in his short career. Drawing was an essential foundation for the art of painting for him and for many other artists.

John Ruskin (1819-1900) founded the Drawing School in Oxford, England, in 1871. He was one of the most influential writers on art and architecture in the 19th century in Britain. As an artist, he sought to capture forms in nature, believing that drawing encouraged close observation and a deeper understanding of the subject. His drawing school was open to ordinary men and women and not specifically intended for training artists. By following his carefully directed course of lessons of copying works of art and drawing from nature, everyday people could enhance their appreciation of art and nature.

For Henry Moore (1898-1986), drawings were frequently a preliminary necessity for sculpting, a way of developing ideas more quickly than creating modeling in three dimensions.

In spite of everything, I shall rise again: I will take up my pencil, which I have forsaken in my great discouragement, and I will go on with my drawing.   - Vincent van Gogh

The development of perspective

In the Middle Ages, the period before the Renaissance, most art in Europe featured figures devoted to Christian worship. Artists painting these pictures left the background to the imagination, for the most part, instead applying metallic gold as a background color. As people gradually became more interested in and aware of the world around them, landscapes and buildings began to appear in paintings, and paintings related more to viewers of the painting rather than the glorification of religious subjects.

An essential artistic problem of the Renaissance became how to paint landscapes and buildings in pictures so that they looked the same as in real life. Linear perspective was the solution: the idea that converging lines meet at a single vanishing point and that all shapes get smaller in all directions with increasing distance from the eye.

The discovery of perspective is attributed to the architect Filippo Brunelleschi (1377-1446). He worked out a system that explained how objects in a painting or drawing are reduced in size according to their position and distance from the eye. The theory was first presented in 1435 when Leon Battista Alberti (1404-1472) provided a system of measurements in paintings. The effects of this were enormous. Although most artists painting in Europe after 1435 were aware of the principles, far from bursting full-fledged onto the Renaissance scene in the first quarter of the 15th century, the understanding of the intricacies of perspective took time to develop and was reached only gradually over a period of 400 years.

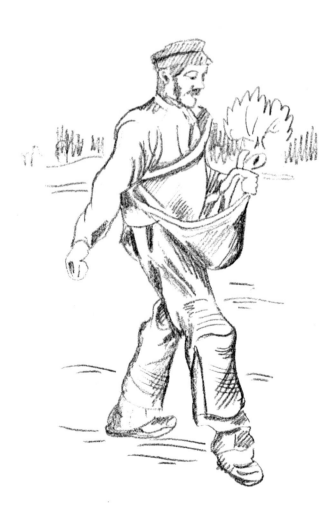

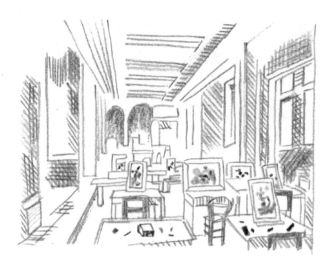

The activity of drawing

Drawing is an activity in which visual information is processed and transformed onto a flat surface. It is a process in which the observer is teaching her eye to really observe and to put down onto paper what she has observed. The observer looks, sees and transfers what she has seen through her hands to the paper surface. And in order to draw well, the eye has to be trained to see well.

The processing of visual information is different from the usual way in which information is processed. It is the special properties of the brain that enable us to draw pictures of our perceptions.

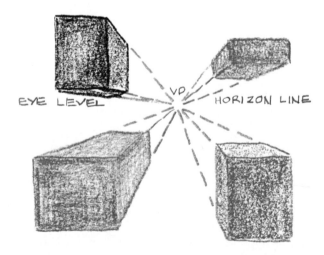

Right and left hemispheres of the brain

Much research and study has been done on how the brain works. The brain can be divided into two halves—the right and left hemispheres. The right brain is connected to the left side of the body and the left brain is connected to the right side. Recent brain research shows that, of the two hemispheres, it is the right hemisphere that perceives and processes visual information. With the right hemisphere we see how things exist in space, understand metaphors, see things in our mind's eye, and can create new combinations of ideas. With the left hemisphere we analyze, abstract, count, mark time, plan step-by-step procedures, verbalize and make rational statements containing logic.

Teaching to the left

Much of our educational system has been designed to cultivate the left hemisphere mode—the verbal, rational, on-time aspect of our consciousness. Teaching focuses on sequences of numbers, rows of seats in the classroom, bells that ring on the exact hour. So, what is happening to the other half of children's brains—spatial imagination, perception and intuition?

Teaching to the whole brain

Educators are realizing that skills developed through right-brain activity are valuable and that, overall, a balance of whole-brain activity is the most desirable. In her book *Drawing on the Right Side of the Brain*, Betty Edwards states that there are two aspects of learning, and that each is valuable to the whole of education.

She notes that "perhaps now that neuroscientists have provided a conceptual base for the right-brain training, we can begin to build a school system that will teach the whole brain. Such a system will surely include training in drawing skills—an efficient, effective way to gain access to right-brain functions." Using the right hemisphere, we are able to draw pictures of our perceptions. In the right-brain mode of information processing, we use intuition and insights, which lead us to exclaim: "Ah, now I've got the picture!" The teaching of drawing skills in the curriculum can be an efficient and effective way to gain access to right-brain functions.

Educating with the whole brain

In her postscript, Betty Edwards mentions David Galin, who points out that one of the tasks of teachers is to train both hemispheres. It is important to activate the verbal, symbolic, logical left hemisphere that has always been trained in traditional education, but also to activate the spatial, relational, holistic right hemisphere.

Another task is to train students to bring both hemispheres to bear on problems in an integrated manner. Edwards recommends using the chalkboard, not just to write words but also to draw pictures and diagrams. Ideally, all information should be presented in at least two modes—verbal and pictorial.

Edwards believes the key to learning is the artist's mode of seeing, to direct attention towards visual information that the left brain cannot or will not process. Always try to present the brain with a task the left brain will refuse, and allow the right brain to use its capacity for drawing.

Visual/spatial learners

From recent cognitive research, Howard Gardner of Harvard has identified seven distinct intelligences and documented the extent to which students possess different kinds of minds and therefore learn, remember, perform and understand in different ways. According to his theory of multiple intelligences,

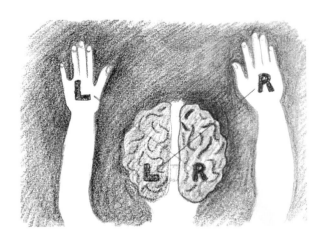

"we are all able to know the world through language, logical-mathematical analysis, spatial representation, musical thinking, the use of the body to solve problems or to make things, an understanding of other individuals and an understanding of ourselves." He identified several different learning styles, one of them the visual/spatial. Visual learners, such as architects and sailors, think in terms of physical space and are very aware of their environments. They like to draw, do jigsaw puzzles, read maps, daydream. They can be taught through drawings and verbal and physical imagery.

Keeping the left side "out of it"

Drawing a perceived form is largely a right-brain function. The left brain, the dominant half, must be kept "out of it." This brings about a state of mind where one becomes less conscious of the passage of time. There is a relaxation of confidence and alertness. This is one of the most wonderful aspects of the right hemisphere mode—the timelessness we experience when sitting down to draw. An hour can easily go by and feel like only five minutes has elapsed. It can be a startling experience when the time allotted for drawing is up and it is time to transition to another activity. Drawing can lead us into a dream-consciousness state, from which it is often difficult to emerge.

Creating right-brain conditions

Varying the conditions in the classroom is an important concern. Talking among students or constant talking by a teacher locks students fairly rigidly into a left-brain mode. A strong shift to the right-brain mode will create a rare condition called silence, or silence can create the potential for right-brain activity. Not only will students be silent; they will be engaged in the tasks at hand. They will be attentive and confident, alert and content.

Shifting to the R-mode

In characterizing the right-brain state of consciousness, Betty Edwards writes: "The R mode is indeed pleasurable, and in that mode you can draw well. The additional advantage of shifting to

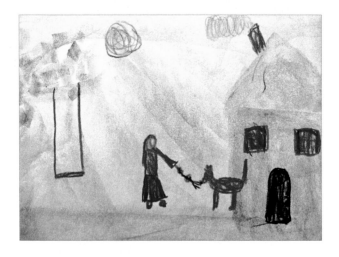

R-B mode is the release, for a time, from the verbal, symbolic domination of the L-mode, a welcome relief. The pleasure may come from resting the left hemisphere and stopping its chatter, keeping it quiet for a change."

This yearning to quiet the left brain may partially explain centuries-old practices such as meditation and self-induced altered states of consciousness. Drawing in right-brain mode induces a changed state of consciousness that can last for hours.

Visualizing and imaging

Both visualizing and imaging are important components of the skill of drawing. To draw is to hold a series of mental images in memory and then transfer them bit by bit to the paper. Edwards calls it "imaging in the R-mode," and she sets up exercises to demonstrate the power of imaging as a device for understanding and remembering complex information. These preliminary exercises are an aid to understanding the instructions that follow throughout the book and are invaluable to the serious drawing student.

Other aspects

Edwards also talks about many other useful aspects in relationship to the right and left hemispheres and how they cross over and connect to our hands. She talks about the duality of human nature and how the right and left sides of our brain and body are embedded in our culture.

She mentions left-handedness and its connection to the right hemisphere, and the connotations of good and not good connected to each side. All in all, *Drawing on the Right Side of the Brain* is excellent reading and highly recommended for further study.

Drawing as a pleasurable activity

Drawing can be a favorite "thing to do," especially for the young child. Rarely do you hear, "I don't like drawing" because drawing is a natural activity, especially up to the age of ten. Children naturally gravitate to putting a mark on a piece of paper without too much forethought. Drawing brings about a real feeling of pleasure, a sense of satisfaction, a sense of well-being. A drawing is often made as a gift to a mom or dad, friend or teacher.

Observing young children drawing

Watching children draw is a pleasure! It is fascinating to watch the process of how they begin and end, to see the content and its placement, the story the drawing tells. Children slowly develop their own unique style, which evolves as they grow through adolescence into adulthood. Some adults leave drawing behind for many years, to discover it again one day.

Sketching on vacation

Enormous pleasure can be derived from sketching while on vacation, such as sitting in front of a cathedral and drawing one of the sculptured figures at the side of an entrance. The whole experience of traveling can be enhanced through taking some time to rest quietly on a bench or stone. Sketching landscapes or buildings brings about a closer connection to nature and the surroundings. The high out-of-reach steeples can be "touched by the eyes" and brought down onto the flat paper, to treasure and remember long after returning home.

Leaving drawing behind

Some adults leave drawing behind altogether. They may have come to the conclusion that they cannot draw and so have consciously or unconsciously avoided drawing since they were young students in the elementary grades. This aspect will be explored in greater detail, as it plays a very important part in how a teacher gains confidence in his/her skills in drawing with children.

Drawing basics

An essential starting point for teaching drawing is a basic knowledge of the elements of drawing.

The page

White paper can be seen as an image of infinite possibility. It holds the mystery of what is to come, of what is to be created. It can also be the cause of much anxiety. A blank piece of paper can be a formidable starting point.

A white page set out on the table in front of you creates an immediate focus—a spatial orientation on a flat surface.

Children will ask for paper, or they will write and draw on other surfaces! Providing the paper will afford opportunities. Young children love paper—whether used for drawing, cutting or gluing.

Imagination

Before you begin to draw, you may already know exactly what you have in mind. On the other hand, you may have no idea of what to do. Imagination is a process of creating images in your mind's eye, leading to expressing the images on paper. Imagination in drawing is a process that can be stimulated and developed in both the young child and the adult.

Imagination as a strong force

Children often begin drawing as early as the second year of life. They start with scribbles, which consist mostly of big loops drawn with a line. At this stage no objects can be recognized in the child's drawing. Gradually, the linear forms evolve into more solid shapes, and forms relating to objects begin to appear.

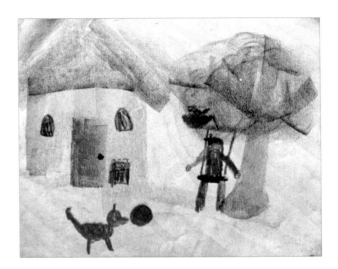

Children's imagination can be powerfully stirred, and each child has her own unique ability to create images. Just as no two children are alike, no two children have the same imagination. Children hearing the same story will "see" the picture before them in their own unique way—and express it differently on the paper.

Each drawing is unique

Even when a teacher guides the children in a drawing, there are many differences in the ways they follow the guidance. They will imitate the drawing that is demonstrated by the teacher in front of the classroom to the best of their ability. They will also add their own touches. With close observation it becomes evident that each drawing has a unique look.

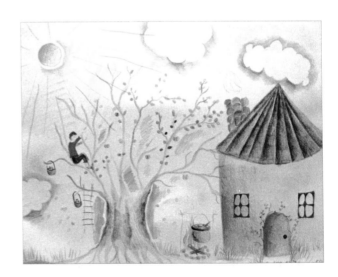

Creativity

Out of this stirring awakening of the imagination, creativity comes about. Sometimes imagination can lie dormant and find its creative expression later, even much later. Often imaginations occur and never see the light of day on paper but are stored away somewhere in mysterious depths.

Love of drawing

Children love to draw and express their imaginations, to explore their own creativity. When they are young this desire is fearless and unrestrained—endless hours of drawing on many pieces of paper happen effortlessly. Often for the adult, creativity is something that does not come readily and needs to be worked at. Adults often need more stimulation and encouragement, especially if they feel or have been told they are not creative, if they have not drawn since childhood, and their creativity and imagination have been lying dormant for many years.

Compositions

To create an original composition requires imagination. It can be an imagination that comes from mysterious depths. Once the imagination is awakened and activated, the components of the imaging need to fit on the page. Together, these components create a composition. The pieces are

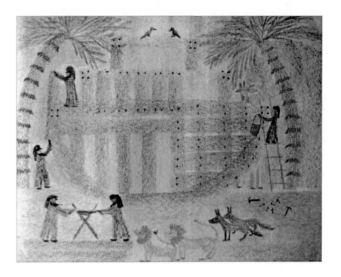

placed on the page; they are brought together to create one piece—a whole, a composition. Through the process of placing the images on paper, a focusing effect is created.

The kindergarten-age child is beginning to get a sense for how objects are placed in the environment and for where objects are to be placed on the page: how tall the figures should be, the height of the tree, the house on the left or right—these are all questions that begin to arise as the child grows and matures.

How to begin

For the teacher, the large, blank, white page can often be so formidable as to have a stifling effect. Creating small sketches helps to stimulate the imaginative process and get the creative juices flowing. The dramatically reduced drawing size is less daunting and can be liberating.

Making small sketches can save time in a busy teacher's life. A drawing that could take up an hour on a larger-sized piece of paper might take only ten minutes on a smaller format, say 5" x 7". It can also be a less frustrating way to prepare a lesson. If the first sketch does not work out, then you have spent only a short amount of time on it. When "starting from scratch," not really knowing what the picture might be, this method can be a real aid in working out compositions. It is easy to enlarge a small sketch to a larger drawing for classroom use.

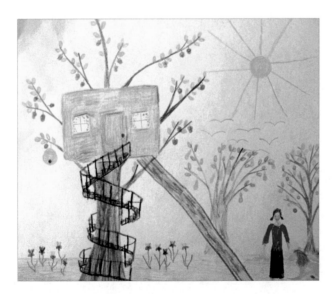

Elements of composition

There are many elements that make up a composition in addition to lines, shapes and forms. Color, tones, and edges where forms meet come into play in the composition.

A balance needs to be created between the various elements. For example, a drawing can have too much yellow, not enough green, too many shades of blue, and so forth. Much of this balancing can be worked out in small sketches. Composing a balanced picture is a skill learned gradually, and the study of composition becomes appropriate only in the middle school years. The students can gradually build up to it, beginning as early as first grade.

Observation drawing as a learning tool

Use drawing as a learning tool. Take students out to draw from nature, such as during a botany block in grade five or studying animals on a farm in third grade. Bring sketches from outside into the classroom and transform them into final illustrations for the main lesson books or other subjects.

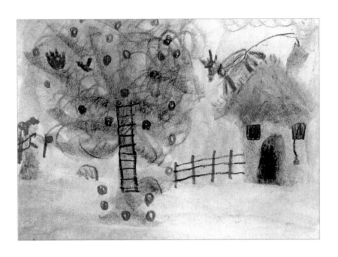

Until they gain forces for observing the world around them, young children are not yet ready to draw from observation. They feel themselves as one with the environment. They gain the ability to step back and observe only when they reach a certain age and begin to feel separate from the world, usually around the age of nine. Until then, drawing is often an unconscious activity and a way for them to express their innermost feelings and impressions of life around them.

Drawing is everything. If somebody contacts me and says, "There is a young sculptor and he's going to be very good—would you like to see his work?" I say, "What's his drawing like?" Oh, he doesn't draw. Well then, he's no good. All the sculptors who have been any good have been great draftsmen. Drawing is enough if you do it well. Lots of great artists do nothing else but draw. I started drawing—unlike sculpting—when I was five or six. Nowadays, I do nothing but draw.

– Henry Moore

Different approaches

*The formation of breathing tones can begin in the early grades.
To teach children to handle stick crayons and colored pencils in so delicate a manner
provides balance to their breathing and circulation, enlivens their imagination
and stimulates their capacities for judgment.*

– Dennis Klocek

There is a wide variety of ways to approach drawing in the classroom.

Linear and contour drawing

The line is the most basic element for creating an image on a surface. This is how young children begin to draw. It begins as a point and moves along in one or several directions until it comes to an end and to rest. It varies in width, widens or narrows or remains constant.

The line as an outline

When a line creates a form, we can think of it as an outline—an outline of a shape that is flat and two-dimensional. The flatness means that we cannot tell from the drawing that it has any depth—nothing comes forward or goes backward, there are no clues as to its three-dimensional quality, its volume.

Two and three dimensions

Two-dimensional is what we can call "flat." There is no suggestion of roundness or of volume. We can

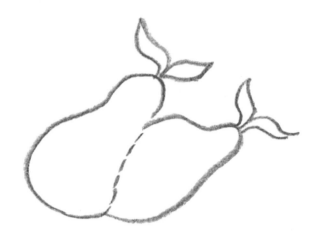

say it has only one plane—it is flat and has no volume. Form and volume are dependent upon all three dimensions—length, width and thickness. Think of form as the three-dimensional shape of volume. A drawing in three dimensions portrays the shape and form as though you could walk around it, as though it is a sculptural form. It has a front, a back and sides.

Contour lines

Contour lines portray a shape or form in a more three-dimensional way than a silhouette. There are additional lines around the shape that come forward or go back to indicate its three-dimensional quality. It is the simplest way to draw shapes and forms that show the bare essentials for recognition by the eye.

In the first figure two pears are shown as two shapes melded into one, without any clues as to their roundness, or as to which pear is lying in front. In the second figure the same pears are rendered in contour with an added line to separate them. The difference between the two figures is slight but significant.

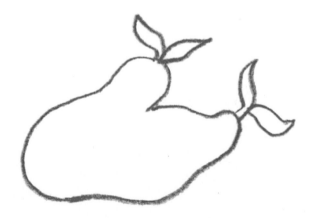

Line as gesture, as movement

A line can be used to create a gesture. In many cave drawings, lines are used in a very expressive manner, capturing the essence of an animal or human form through movement. The line also needs to be a moving, sweeping line, to convey the essence of the movement.

Linear form as weightless

Linear forms, no matter how complex, have no volume. They are flat, two-dimensional forms. They do not come forward or go backward, or go up or down—they are movements on a flat plane. Even when they are engraved into a surface, such as carved into a stone, they remain weightless.

Form drawing: through the ages

Drawing forms with lines is one of the oldest art forms of mankind. From the Neolithic and Bronze Age stone carvings to the Lombard and Celtic arts, the form made through line has played a very important part in humanity's journey of art. Over several thousands of years, hands have been busy imprinting surfaces with linear forms—drawing, painting or carving—for pure decoration or for conveying messages. Linear forms range from the basic straight line to the very complicated woven ribbon forms of Celtic art (see "Form drawing").

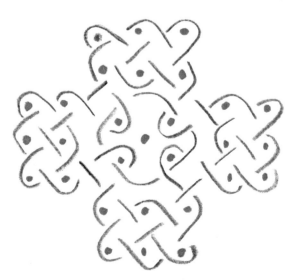

Sculptural drawing

One of the easier ways to understand what it means to portray an object or a person is to think of what is before you as a sculpted form. A sculpted form is modeled out of substance that has weight and that has three dimensions—a front and back, a base and top, and sides. It can be a form that is round like a ball (convex), hollow like a cave (concave), or angular like a cube (planes with flat sides), or a form that is a combination of convex, concave and planes. Angular, hard three-dimensional forms are found in the mineral shapes of crystals. Soft, round planes are found everywhere in the plant, animal and human kingdoms.

The use of modeling

Modeling forms is helpful to understanding the three-dimensional world. Working with a modeling medium in the hands, using the eyes and fingers together to touch and feel the making of a form, is an excellent exercise. The solidity and weight of the form can really be experienced as well as its dimensions.

Drawing as a sculptor

Three-dimensional drawing and sculpting are closely connected. Many sculptors begin the creative process of forming shapes by drawing first. Henry Moore, the British sculptor, loved to draw the sheep that grazed on the hills around his estate. He knew that to draw is to see. The activity of drawing stimulated his creative forming process.

Likewise, sculpting stimulates the drawing process and helps the drawer to come to a closer understanding of what she wants to portray on paper. Drawing a form on a flat piece of paper and shading it to look three-dimensional creates an illusion.

Creating the illusion

Begin with the simple example of a sphere. First, draw a circle with a single line. Observe its flatness, its lack of solidity, its lack of roundness.

Now draw a circle, but instead of a line to indicate the outer edge, add a tone, draw a textured surface. The tone is a medium blue and is the same over the

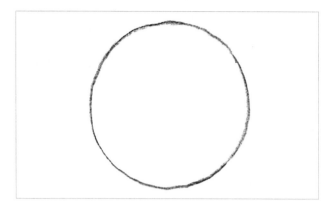

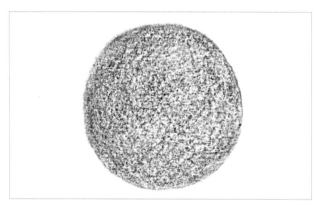

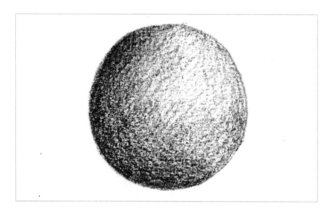

out and picking the object up from the paper. Or, if we have created a landscape or still life, we may feel that we could step forward and move into the picture. The ultimate is when we feel ourselves in the picture—we are there.

Light and dark

Light can be thought of as the overcoming of darkness. Our eyes are unable to see the world and its multiple forms and shapes without light. Darkness is the absence of light.

Light shining on forms

Light falling on a form allows us to visually determine its shape and size. Wherever light is unable to reach a hidden space, darkness is created. The shirt on a hanger is drawn in line, flat and without tone, yet you can see the folds and get some sense of how they drape. In the illustration below (right), the lines are still there, but an added tone blends in and softens the lines. Shadows are created by dark tones applied to the areas that the light cannot reach.

Soft and hard edges of shadows

Observation of a shirt hanging fairly close to a window will show you how light is unable to penetrate into areas which are receded. The further back the fold, the greater the absence of light, and

entire sphere. Looking at this sphere, we can begin to get a sense of solidity, but we still cannot determine whether the sphere has a front, a back or density.

The third drawing shows a differentiation of tone. By developing a darker tone on one side of the sphere, we can begin to get a feeling of its roundness, that it is a sphere.

Look back at the first two drawings and note the distinct difference. The illusion has been created. The illusion can be so real that we may feel like reaching

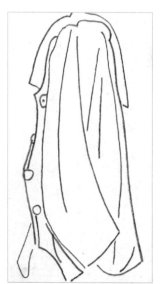
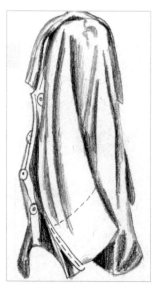

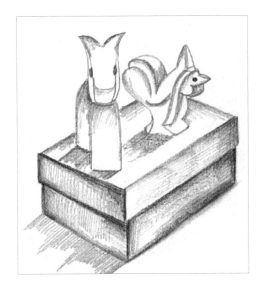

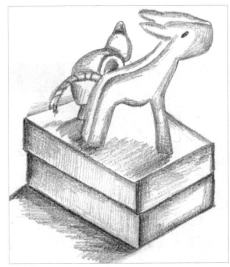

the darker the shadow. Look even closer and you can see that some of the edges of the shadows are soft. They gently and gradually transition to the light but others abruptly end in sharp edges. There is much to be observed!

Edges of forms

In observing a form, we can see the front, the top and perhaps a side, but from any one point of view we cannot simultaneously see the front, sides, base, top and back, unless the object is made of glass and is transparent.

How does an edge arise?

An edge arises at just the point where what you are observing disappears from view. You are able to see this edge because the light is shining on its surface and perhaps the outer edge is a different color or tone than what lies behind it. If you move a few steps to the left, the edge changes. You now see more of what you could not see before on the left side, but more will be hidden from your view on the right side.

The illustrations above are of an identical composition of a box with wooden animals, but drawn from different points of view. The drawing on the left is of one view of the box, showing the rooster from a side view, and the fawn can be seen from the front only. The light source is coming from the right, and all the surfaces have tones, ranging from very light to dark.

The illustration above right shows a view further around to the left. The fawn is most easily recognizable shown here in a side view, and the rooster has turned its back on it all and is mostly obscured.

The shifting of the viewpoint caused new edges to arise and former edges to disappear. You could say the edges have vanished because they never really were there in the first place!

Tones

Tone is the term used for a color appearing on a surface. For example, drawing with a pencil on a piece of paper creates a "tone." A tone can have many variations. A dark tone can have a distinct border and come to an abrupt end. Or a tone can have no edges, no borders, and no lines around it. A tone can move from dark to light and back again to dark. It can be kept so non-differentiated that it is hard to tell where it begins and ends.

Working with existing masterpieces

Learning from the masters can be a rich and valuable practice when learning to draw. There is so much to observe in every drawing and painting. Just observing is an art all by itself.

All kinds of works of art can be studied, analyzed and copied. A black and white etching can be copied but rendered in color, such as *Melancholia,* an engraving by the German artist Albrecht Dürer.

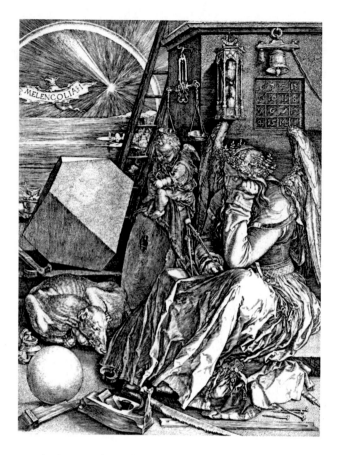

along and change as the story unfolds and finally ends. This is a process of movement of the imagination. When the student puts pencil to paper, one or several images in the story will appear, transcribed from what was originally seen in the imagination. You can also think of this as a "living movement of imagination" come to rest.

Diagonal shading

Diagonal-shaded drawing can be beneficial to many people in these modern days. It promotes powers of concentration. Rudolf Steiner said it helps the ego to incarnate and work in the physical in the right way. It is therefore especially beneficial to young people and teenagers. It helps to link thinking, feeling and willing; head, heart and hands. — G.A.M. Knapp

Using diagonal shading (also known as slant line technique) for drawing is not merely unusual but also unique, and can be therapeutic and liberating. It is

Works by Rembrandt can be studied for his extraordinary ability to create glowing light around the subjects and scenes he depicted.

A "ready made" outline or contour

Giving students a piece of paper with an image in contour with empty space inside gives them the possibility of filling in the space with color. As mentioned earlier, this is a favorite pastime for the young child as he or she delights in "coloring in." The image has already been provided and it is relaxing to color it in. The images are "ready made," and do not call on and develop the image-making powers of a child.

Drawing as creative expression

Another approach is to create from scratch. Have a blank piece of paper and a pencil ready on the table. A singular effort needs to take place—that of creating the image. When hearing a story, a student forms inner pictures and images in her mind that move

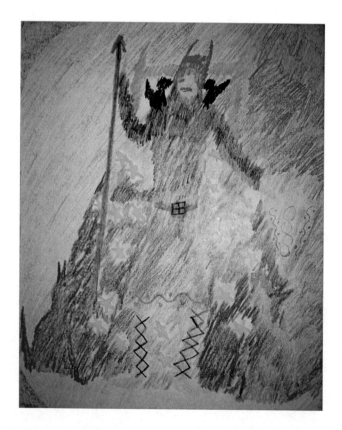

unique in that it is not well known in the art world and is not an established approach to drawing. It is therapeutic in that it can be an "artistic gateway" for people who need to strengthen their sense of self. It can be liberating for adults who have not experienced artistic work beyond the outline and linear methods of drawing. It can be used in the classroom for students in the elementary grades through high school and beyond.

Introduction

Assya Turgeniev developed the technique of black-on-white diagonal-shaded drawing during the building of the first Goetheanum in the early 20th century. A monumental building, the Goetheanum was designed by Rudolf Steiner for the purposes of artistic and spiritual work. The Goetheanum included carved columns of wood and engraved glass windows.

Turgeniev was a trained glass engraver and developed the diagonal-shaded drawing technique from her experience of working with Steiner on the windows. In her book, *The Goetheanum Windows,* she describes Steiner's explanation of his theory and the practice of glass engraving. The windows can be seen today in the second Goetheanum in Dornach. They are radiant in magnificent colors, with etched lines that allow the light to shine through with varied intensity.

Darkness and light

In his book *Darkness and Light,* G.A.M. Knapp describes the slanted line method and technique, giving suggestions for materials as well as providing many exercises to work with. The first exercises begin with learning the technique, keeping the strokes consistently diagonal at a 45-degree angle and straight, from top right to bottom left of the page. Once the method has been practiced and the technique of the diagonal stroke has become familiar, further exercises can be worked on, such as learning to transition from darkness to light and from light to darkness.

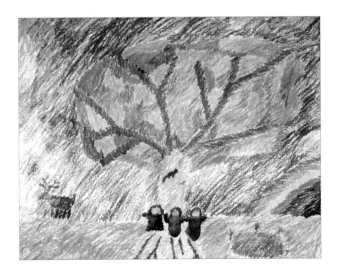

Forms arising from the interplay of light and dark

Light has a tendency to expand, to appear larger, but shade has an inward, diminishing effect. The expanding quality of light tends to strive upward, while dark can be felt as a contracting force that drags down into gravity.

– Rudolf Steiner

Knapp suggests it is best to begin with the kingdoms of nature and the four elements of earth, water, fire and air. He provides many illustrations and suggestions for exercises, including the human face, figure and landscapes. Many of the exercises, such as people sitting around a campfire, can be taken up in the middle school.

Alternative to the line

In the introduction to her book *Black and White Shaded Drawing,* Valerie Jacobs writes, "Although great beauty has been achieved by line drawing in the past, this new approach leads us more into the future. By avoiding the line, one is left free to enter into the living qualities of light and dark in as natural a way as we breathe; in this way we leave room for the playing in of inspiration." Jacobs further points out that this method makes other demands on a student beyond observation and representation through line. It can be regarded as an alternative to orthodox methods of

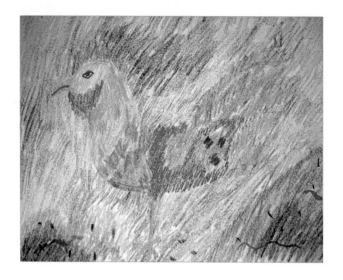

drawing. If the exercises are approached with an open mind and done step by step, they will create an inner transformation in the student, and a whole new world of possibilities will open up for her.

The technique in the classroom

The diagonal-shaded drawing technique is a wonderful approach to work in the classroom. Invariably, students are prone to drawing with outlines, and often very strong ones. This works for a few who are uniquely talented and can accurately create realistic depictions of recognizable shapes and forms. But for most children it is a struggle, beyond the ages of nine and ten, to draw what they see with accuracy.

When to introduce the technique

Some remedial teachers feel that children as young as age 7 should begin their drawing instruction in first grade with the slant line, as opposed to using the beeswax blocks. It is also possible to introduce this technique beginning in fourth grade, an ideal time as students transition from drawing with beeswax blocks and sticks to drawing with colored pencils. Transitioning from the broad painterly strokes made with blocks to shading with pencils is a big leap. Drawing with the beeswax sticks in slanted, diagonal lines is a midway point between broad and wide painterly crayons and sharp, thin pencils. Typically, students who are used to drawing with blocks will, when given pencils in fourth grade, tend to hurry

their drawing, especially the background, and create scratchy surface tones.

Note: There are differing opinions on when this technique should be introduced. In some Waldorf schools, slant line drawing is not taken up until the high school years. Since many schools do not go further than the first eight grades, it is up to the teacher to study the approach and consider its potential merits in the elementary classroom.

Other advantages

Students in fourth grade are excited to learn new techniques and the slanted line technique can become a rite of passage as students rise through the grades. This gives them something to look forward to and to prepare them for eventual "shading." They are ready for the next phase beyond the broad surface of the crayons and are looking ahead at drawing in their books with colored pencils.

More importantly, this method gives the student an opportunity to create form through color or dark and light, rather than the line and the sharp edge. Colors can blend into each other and make the edges of the forms less defined. Drawings can take on a more impressionistic look rather than a stark, linear, graphic look. This can be freeing and helpful for the nine-year-old who yearns for "realistic" interpretation of forms on the canvas. It can also be very freeing for adults who have not drawn since elementary grades and lack self-confidence in their drawing abilities.

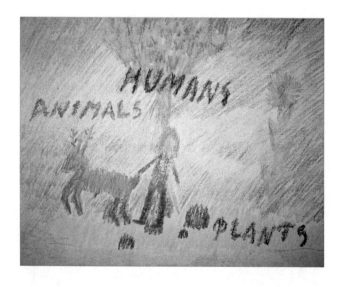

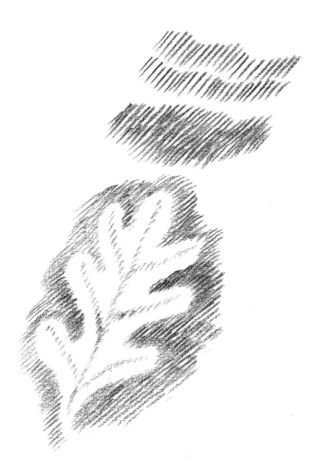

It is best in the early grades not to demand the lifting of the hand with each stroke. It is more important that the child enjoy the technique and find the results rewarding and satisfying. Keeping the hand down on the page allows the student to move back and forth diagonally in a more relaxed manner. Each stroke does not require the same effort. When the hand is not lifted after each stroke, the slanted lines are connected by the upward stroke from below left to top right. This tends to give the strokes a more closed-up impression with less, if any, white space in between.

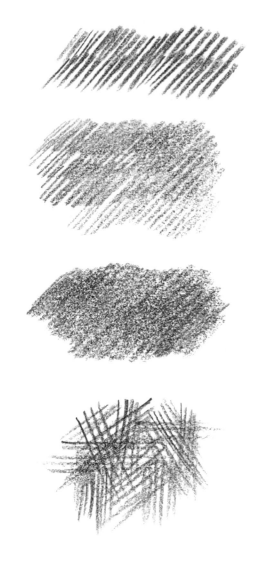

The strokes

The method outlined by both Knapp and Jacobs calls for the strokes to be individual, to be made "consciously" from beginning to end. The impact should be firm and decisive; the release should be gradual and controlled.

It is a considerable challenge for the fourth grader to lift the hand continuously after each stroke. This requires a very deliberate and conscious movement repeated many times in one drawing. Many students will find it hard to keep lifting the hand at the end of each stroke, but some students will take to it fairly easily.

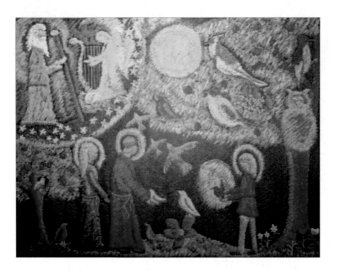

Working with colors

In addition to working in black and white, the diagonal shading lends itself beautifully to colors blending into and over one another. Shapes are clearly formed but have "breathing" edges. When the strokes are very evenly drawn and of the same length, the drawing can have the appearance of needlepoint, as though the strokes are slanted stitches. A broad base of color drawn with block crayons can also be worked over with slanted lines. For the teacher, drawing with the slant line on the board is a special treat, and the students appreciate its special quality.

The temperaments

In her book, *The Temperaments and the Arts,* Magda Lissau writes that diagonal shading provides a harmonious interplay of all three soul forces— thinking, feeling and willing, and children are ready to work with this technique by age ten. "The feeling element is addressed by the interweaving of the strokes; the will element is engaged by the effort to keep the strokes even and the same length and to keep them separate from each other. The thinking element is addressed by the forms that arise or that one intends to put on the paper." Lissau points out that "the temperaments reveal themselves through their language of form, color and intensity." She goes on to describe how the temperament of the student expresses itself in the size, organization, and boldness of the strokes and the different colors used.

Drawing forms

For the ten-year-old who draws animals and humans, the slant line affords an opportunity to render shapes and forms in a less realistic way than forms with a distinct outline. Instead of spending a lot of time trying to "get it just right," the student can draw the animal with the slanted strokes without attention to exact details. For the teacher who is still learning to draw shapes and forms, this can be a great way to build confidence.

"Finding the form" through the interplay of light and dark or different colors is ideal for "exploring around" with the crayon/pencil on the paper and creating form. Some students who prefer to draw stark graphic images will feel the challenge of this freer approach to finding form.

Unique beauty

Diagonal-shaded drawings offer a unique method of creating beauty in both black and white and color. It is a great way to prepare students for shaded drawing in the middle school years. In "shading," the strokes blend and create a more continuous and blended overall tone with the direction of the strokes less defined, such as in cross-hatching.

Drawing with a breathing tone

A breathing tone is alive with possibility. The texture of it has a quality to it that is flexible and alive in contrast to a hard, impenetrable dense tone. Dennis Klocek writes in *Drawing from the Book of Nature:* "The artist concerned with the living qualities of light is interested in tones, tonal gradations and atmosphere—not so much the surface details but the harmonious shapes within the forms."

To shade is to apply shadow to three-dimensional objects, to create the illusion of volume. Shading consists of tones varying in degrees of intensity or darkness. Klocek describes this tone as a breathing tone, a tone that should not have a definitive edge. He indicates that it is most satisfactorily made by a rhythmic stroke moving back and forth in a diagonal direction from upper right to lower left and back again. "A breathing tone is a tone that can as easily become a flower as a cloud or change from a circle to a triangle to a square."

Exercises

Klocek gives numerous examples of how to draw with a breathing tone and apply this approach to drawing nature in all its forms, including both the plant and animal worlds and some references to landscapes.

He uses the leaf as an example. He first draws a branch with leaves in contour lines that give the illusion of three dimensions. "Lines occur in nature only in very specific places along edges where planes meet, or in stems of plants where the light is active." Klocek moves beyond contour drawing towards a more "painterly" work. The line imposes too strict an edge and "any spontaneity with color or brush is restricted." It is preferable to work with tones where edges arise out of intensification of tones when they meet.

He gives exercises in working with tones and recommends continuous practice until the drawing student can create breathing tones that can easily become light or dark and have the flexibility to metamorphose into any form. Furthermore he shows how a tone can find its shape and that seeking and finding rhythm in the effort can be very therapeutic.

Application in the classroom

Shading with a breathing tone does not need much introduction after the students have worked with the diagonal-shading technique. In some ways it is a less exacting technique, as there can be more freedom in the direction of the rhythmic strokes. However, it takes time, effort and patience for a student to master the skill of shading with smooth tones, especially with large areas of tones, such as the sky and large expanses of landscape. The lack of interesting features in large surfaces makes for an impatient student who wants to get it completed as quickly as possible.

Beginning exercises

It is a good idea to start the students off with some of Klocek's recommendations for beginning exercises before moving on to form. Do exercises with shape gestures using circles and ovals that metamorphose into egg and drop shapes. He suggests varying the drop shapes and notes that the drop and its related shapes are very common in the world of plants, particularly in the leaf.

Drawing the leaf

In a botany main lesson, drawing plants is a great opportunity to work specifically on tone technique and to avoid linear contour renderings. Using a simplified version of Klocek's leaf drawing exercise, we can begin with creating the entire leaf shape first, rather than first creating an overall tone on the page and then "bringing the leaf out of the tone."

Starting with the stem, create a tone that begins to establish the leaf shape as though slowly revealed, as though a film is being removed from an image that is already there. Imagine a generic leaf shape and create this shape with a light tone. Moving the pencil back and forth over the paper, the shape can be adjusted as it grows into its final form. This can be a great advantage to the student as the shape can be worked on until perfected, as opposed to creating the form with lines that may often need to be erased until it looks right.

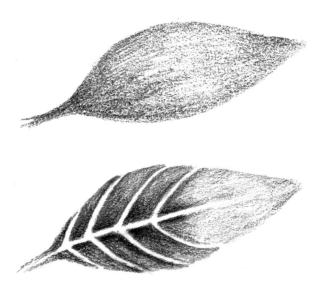

Creating the veins

While the mid-vein stays in mind at all times, darker tones can be applied to the areas between the veins to make them stand out. This approach creates the veins in "negative space." Think of this as opposite to drawing the leaf as an outline with veins drawn in.

This is a challenging approach and takes a lot of focus, imagination and effort by the students and commitment by the teacher. Once the veins have been established, adding a background can enhance the leaf image. An application of a tone around the edges, leaving a light-filled margin all around, can be very effective and make the leaf seem as if it is alive and even hovering above the surface.

Other exercises

There are many wonderful exercises in *Drawing from the Book of Nature,* and it is full of beautiful drawings of insects, animals, trees and plants. Klocek delves into the studies of gestures and shapes and makes recommendations for motifs for the early grades, such as a bird. He shows how the bird is often the shape of an egg. "By drawing an egg as a tonal shape, we can begin to see the bird-like qualities immediately."

He emphasizes that caution should be taken with the young child in employing sophisticated methods of representation. In his opinion, direct copying of natural objects can harden the imaginative process in later life. "The purpose of the exercises is to develop a sensitivity to living tones as an artistic tool." This artistic tool, once learned, can be applied to all the illustrations in the main lesson books, as well as any drawing activity where the application of varied tones enhance the images. Until they learn object drawing in the middle school years, children are better off drawing in their own way rather than trying to realistically portray the exact details of an object.

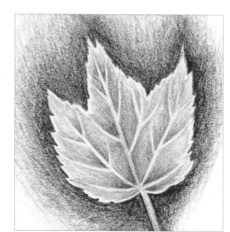

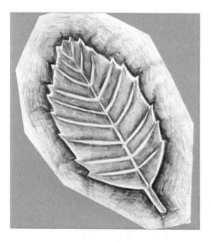
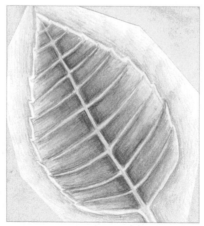

Form drawing
A powerful force in education

by Arthur Auer

The Waldorf curriculum placed two new artistic activities into the service of education: eurythmy, a new art of dance movement, and form drawing, an active form of geometry for children. This happened at the beginning of the 20th century when a new consciousness of art was freeing the elements of line, color and form from always having to depict reality naturalistically. As the Russian abstract painter Kandinsky proclaimed,

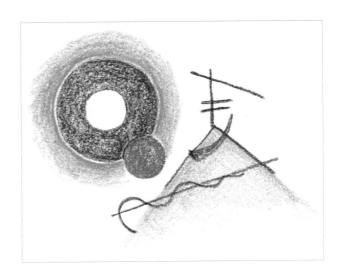

The line is a thing [with a] practical function like a chair... and this thing ... has its own sound. When in the picture a line is freed from designating something else and functions as itself, then its inner sound is not weakened by being in a secondary role and it receives its full inner power.

Form drawing releases the power of pure line and resonates formatively in the soul, nervous system and brain of the doer. This action geometry is an excellent non-intellectual preparation of the inner physical and mental capacities of young children for later intellectual work with geometric imaging and relates to higher cortical function. It builds the neural foundation of a mobile thinking that can grasp process, metamorphosis and whole systems.

Teaching form drawing

In order for you as teacher to bring form drawing to your children, you need to grow to love doing it yourself as a recreation, as a re-creating of yourself and the fabric of your inner life. The German poet and scientist Goethe once pointed out that each

thing and its form we look at with care creates an inner organ in us. Regular practice and involvement with a form, even if for only five minutes a day, can bring noticeable inner results after a series of three or more days. Think of it as a kind of enjoyable cosmic doodling! The intervening nights allow the form to sink in and become a more permanent part of you and the woven patterns of your mind. Such a prior routine is a good way for a teacher to prepare to bring a form to students. When you go to the blackboard to demonstrate a form, it will stream out of you through your hand.

I experience that form drawing, above all, has the effect of centering and ordering the soul and mind. It allows one to rhythmically practice maintaining one's inner center and balance while at the same time being engaged in a process of dynamic movement, flow and tension. This is a valuable capacity to develop for life and especially for teaching.

Form drawing is, in fact, an excellent activity for adults as well as for school children. It strengthens the human ego, self-control, and vitality in anyone who rhythmically practices it. Rudolf Kutzli has designed three beautiful books of *Form Drawing: Workbooks I, II, III* to help adults gain a lasting and meditative relationship to this special art. To assist teachers in coming into the right frame of mind about form drawing I created a verse for contemplation (inspired by the words of the sculptor Carl Kemper):

> *In thinking and in doing*
> *I become one with the Line.*
> *I feel differently, not about it*
> *But within it,*
> *Its form, its gesture,*
> *Its quality, its journey.*
> *I slip inside the life of Line,*
> *Moved, renewed,*
> *Centered.*

Archetypal forms arising out of organic body movement

Young children love to engage in life-filled movement and instinctively sense how form drawing makes it visible. The first wonderful scribbling of two- and three-year-olds arises out of their eagerness for motion and a delight in seeing it make its mark on paper. In early childhood, the most archetypal of organic movements and linear forms (circle, cross, spiral, and so forth) appear in children's playful activity. Michaela Strauss documents these motifs in her excellent research book, *Understanding Children's Drawings*. Teachers should study these forms as indications of what children need to draw on a more sophisticated level in the early elementary grades. Another related and valuable research study is that of Sylvia Fein called *First Drawings: Genesis of Visual Thinking*. In it is a wealth of ancient and primitive rock drawings side by side with pictures by very young children. The similarities are stunning.

Resources to inspire you to create your own forms

There is a wonderful course of exercises that takes up many of these early archetypal forms on a formal school age level. Laura Embry-Stine and Ernst Schuberth's *Form Drawing: Grades One through Four* is a superb guidebook to motifs that appropriately engage the forces of living imagination. To supplement this manual, a new teacher should also have *Form Drawing* by Margaret Frohlich and Hans Niederhauser. This book is a source of many more forms as well as the pedagogical reasons for doing various forms at different grade levels (see special bibliography of form drawing sources and many of Rudolf Steiner's indications on p. 131). Guidebooks, however, provide seed examples that should start to grow in you and stimulate your own image-forming capacities. They should not replace or hinder the growth of your own creativity. As you gain more experience and momentum, design new forms and offshoots to suit your students and various situations. You can, of course, keep collecting the forms of others and trying them out. But as soon as possible, take the plunge and exercise and expand your own inner powers of imagination.

Movement captured and brought to rest in form

Form drawing is actually the activity of capturing part of a movement flow in even, flat "smudges" sculpturally applied on paper. It records the traces of a movement pattern that grazes the surface, makes its mark and is brought to rest. It is a snapshot of something bigger and full of energy and spirit. Children sense the true origin of forms and need to move each one with hands, arms and/or feet and legs before putting them on paper. For example, when you do spirals in grades one through three, precede the act of drawing with combinations of the following movement options:

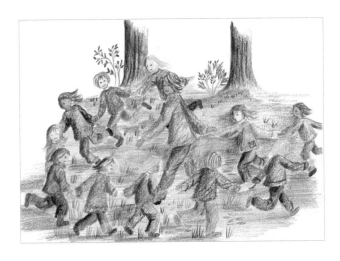

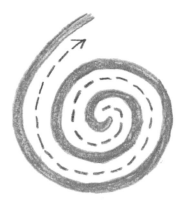

Large motor:

- Join hands and lead the whole group in an inward spiral and then out again: "Let us all go into the little house of snail..."
- Have individual children run large spirals out on the playground and walk smaller ones inside.
- Have them plow huge spirals in the snow if you live in a place that brings snow.

Medium motor:

- Make spirals with the hand in a sand box outside or in the classroom.
- Make large spirals in the air several times with arm, hand and pointer finger.
- Make them on the floor with leg and foot.
- Practice a large one on the blackboard.
- Trace one on a large piece of paper on the desk several times to feel and plan where your final one will go.

Smaller motor:

- Trace a spiral on the back of a neighbor and have him/her reciprocate.

Fine motor:

Finally, take up the stick crayon or soft colored pencil and carefully make the form. Go over it carefully in the same strokes and direction at least two more times and feel the motion that made the form. The motion and process of coming to the form are the main purpose of the activity and affect the child the most. The final visual product on paper is secondary. In general, it is healthiest for young children to go from wide, sweeping gross motor movements to smaller and smaller ones. The form drawing process needs to stir the breathing, senses, circulation and blood! Making a form with a crayon or pencil should be the final intellectual stage of a full experience that engages the child's entire being.

Form stories and pure forms

Some teachers make a connection between certain forms and images in a story or in nature. For example, Curly the Snail inspires the imagination of the children to go into a spiral while saying a verse: "Let us go into the little house of Curly the Snail..."

Or two characters traveling up and down the rolling hills become the undulating curves of a form on paper. In introducing form drawing in first grade, I did this to a limited extent to start the children off and sometimes to excite enthusiasm. Mostly, however, I discovered that the children loved to do pure forms without reference to natural objects and the like. They seem to instinctively sense that forms have their own language and world. Later on, in the middle and upper grades I experienced that their sense of and feeling for form became the foundation for becoming

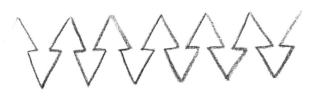

more aware of nature forms and designing beautiful objects in the practical arts (wooden spoons, bowls, knitted patterns and their own clothing) as well as in geometry and higher mathematics!

Demonstrating forms

You can demonstrate a form in chalk on the blackboard or in crayon on paper taped to it or on an easel. Model a balanced flow in your strokes for the children. Going too fast can lead to sloppiness. Going too slowly and painstakingly makes the process too constricting and smacks of intellectual perfectionism. Practice the human middle. The ego centers and strengthens itself best in a healthy tension and gentle oscillation between too fast and too slow.

Rendering forms freely and developing the feeling will

Expect the children to render the forms you demonstrate rather than slavishly copying them with precise, pedantic exactness. This promotes a freer and more relaxed movement and allows room for reasonable variation. This, after all, is freehand geometry! At intervals and with your guidance, have the children make their own designs and share them with each other. Have an individual put hers on the blackboard for all to try.

Above all, make sure children experience feelings of joy and satisfaction each time in your form drawing lessons. Allow them to breathe between listening to step-by-step instructions, concentration and hard work, on the one hand, and lightness and the elation of self-discovery, on the other hand. Keep verbal directions to a minimum. Plan for a lot of absorbed doing, practice and trying out. (Avoid pedantic, rigid lessons that make the children wait too much and frustrate initiative.)

When such absorbed activity is allowed the right time and is not nervously rushed, it helps develop in the child what sculptor Michael Howard calls the *feeling will*. This capacity of the soul allows a human being to connect with and penetrate deeply and actively into life (see Howard, 2002).

Paper, utensils, color, display

Form drawing can be done on all kinds of paper (newsprint, quality drawing paper, and so forth) with pointed stick crayons (grades 1-4) or soft colored pencils (grades 4-5). The application of color is secondary to the main purpose and should not obscure lines or interfere with the harmonious flow of hand movements following the form. For example, to sweep out a beautiful curve and then to thicken it with jagged, scratchy strokes in different directions is counterproductive. To accommodate a child's urge to keep experiencing the dimension of movement, have him carefully go over the form two or more times, perhaps with a yellow to make a red shine more. Then allow him to apply a light surface background evenly by "painting" it with a block crayon color, perhaps a complementary one to the main form (for example a blue form against an orange). Some tricky forms may be mapped out in lemon yellow before applying a darker color.

Many form drawing practice papers in grades 1-3 may be disposed of or sent home for parents to see. At times, pictures can be displayed, but their real value lies mainly in the doing. The cultural motifs of grades 4-5 (Norse, Celtic, Greek, and others) lend themselves more appropriately to display and the permanent decoration (borders, and so forth) of main lesson books.

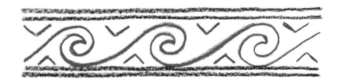

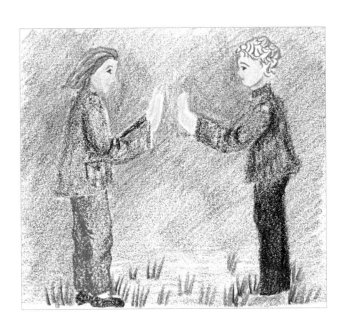

Further examples of movement before drawing and other methods

First, second and third grade Challenge Drawings (vertical mirror forms): The teacher draws a vertical midline in golden yellow on the blackboard and then a form on the left in a color such as orange (see illustration below).

Prior to putting a specific form on paper, partners face each other and take turns using arms and hands to make forms that are mirrored by the other person. This warm-up exercise does not necessarily have to focus on the particular form at hand. It also works for up and down reflections and can even be done in third grade with four people mirroring each other in quadrants. Afterwards, facing and following the teacher's motions, students individually make the vertical line and the specific form in the air with one hand and then its mirror image with the other

several times. Now ask the children to make both sides simultaneously, the right hand mirroring the left. All make a golden midline on the paper and trace the form with the finger on its left side following each direction of the teacher.

Finally, the children render the left form and are challenged to reflect what they draw in a mirror image on the right. (I call these mirror drawings "challenge drawings" because they call on students to find something new and are not always easy to do.) For particularly difficult forms, you may lead them step by step after they have tried themselves (including making the mirror image on the right for them to follow). Leave time for practice and come back to some forms on consecutive days if you can. Mirror forms help the brain practice sorting out sidedness and work against dyslexic reversal tendencies that are natural in many young children.

Knotting rope before fourth grade Norse, Celtic and Lombard form drawings

By fourth and certainly fifth grade, students are not necessarily going through all the preliminary movement exercises listed above, but that does not mean that teachers should stop finding ways to derive forms out of engaging action before the hand takes up the crayon or pencil. The complex Celtic and Norse overlapping weaving patterns that are done in grades 4 and up educate the thinking (following "threads of thought").

Some simple knot forms can be done first in rope. This involves truly thinking with the intelligence of the hands that neurologically helps build the fabric of our brains (Wilson, 1998).

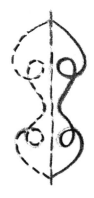

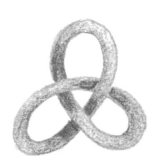
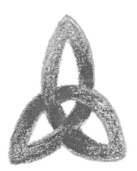

In fifth grade form drawing most often gives way and birth to the freehand geometry of regular figures such as square, triangle, and so forth. Border forms (Greek and others) are still done to decorate the edges of main lesson pages. The Frohlich and Niederhauser *Form Drawing* book has some seed ideas for Greek shields.

Upper grades: Rudolf Kutzli outlines an entire twelve-grade curriculum for form drawing in his *Form Drawing: Workbook II,* and he advocates that it is very good for adults as well.

Form drawing as a formidable tool in the curriculum

Use it generously and regularly:

1. Block: In Europe, form drawing is often done as an entire main lesson block each year in the lower grades. In North America, it is usually the first main lesson block of the first grade and is a prelude to learning to write.

2. Weekly period: Form drawing can be done once a week in an extra main lesson like painting.

3. Ten minutes before main lesson: As children enter the classroom, they can do quick forms. This helps certain children to settle down.

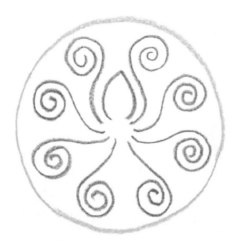

4. Spontaneous therapy: Teachers can decide on the spot that their class needs to do form drawings such as inward spirals to help harmonize them as a group. (Spirals are good for all ages.)

5. Combined in various other blocks: Short form drawing exercises can be inserted in the main lessons of other subject blocks (freehand geometry in grades 4-5 math, for example).

6. Mini-blocks of time: Short practices and exercises can occur for a series of days or weeks at various times (before school, in main lessons, in extra main lessons, before main activities such as reading or math practice).

Kinds of form drawing

The ORIGINAL curriculum form drawings indicated by Rudolf Steiner are mostly single entities that do not tend to repeat themselves in rhythmical sequences: straight lines, curves, circles, spirals, ellipses, angles, symmetry exercises (right/left, up/down), asymmetry figures (three-fold, and so forth), transformations of inner and outer forms, translations from curved to angular, metamorphoses, and so forth.

TEMPERAMENT DRAWINGS: Rudolf Steiner gave forms to meet the needs of the four different temperaments (*Discussions with Teachers IV*). The form for the sanguine is unlike the other three single forms in that it repeats itself rhythmically to help children become centered and calm down.

DYNAMIC DRAWING was developed for therapeutic situations but is also good for all children. It involves repeated ribbon-like sequences (see Kirchner and Jünemann).

HANDWRITING PREPARATION FORMS: Form sequences have been developed that prepare the way for and help artistic writing and penmanship (see Gladich, Clausen).

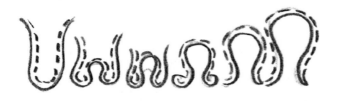

Change and metamorphosis

Central to the purpose of all form drawing is the fact that it involves a formative process arising out of change and growth. A crayon point on the paper expands into a curve into a semicircle into a circle! In mirror drawing, a figure on the left is changed into its opposite on the right.

Furthermore, certain form exercises reveal the special aspect of stage-by-stage transformations or metamorphosis. In contrast to a repetition of the same motif in dynamic form drawing and ribbon patterns, metamorphic sequences show forms that gradually and organically turn from one stage into the next (see illustration) and are each different. Whereas in sculptural modeling you can bring about metamorphosis with one changing object (i.e., a lump of clay), in drawing you can illustrate separate stages and imagine these stand for one changing entity. Both arts are excellent means to exercise a plasticity and freedom of thought and educate process-oriented and whole-systems thinking.

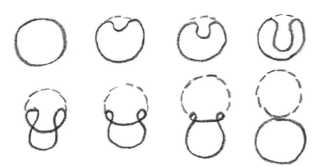

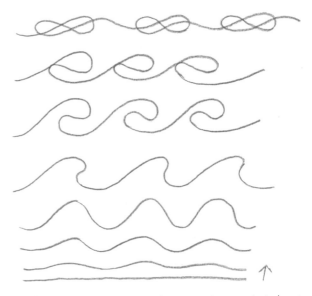

Grades 4–5: Wave progression turns into artistic knot (after Kutzli). Begin at base.

Drawing at different age levels

*The developmental story begins with children as young as twenty-four months,
whose scribbling is considered by many adults to be a meaningless result of muscular activity,
and continues through children of eight years, whose art is commonly viewed as striving
to depict the persons and things around them.*

– Rhoda Kellogg

The developmental story is a fascinating one, and very important for teachers who draw with children. Teachers who have an insight into the development of drawing skills at different age levels will serve the children better as they strive to be accepting of what the children are capable of at any given time on their drawing journey.

A personal history

Each person has a hidden art history, the development of art from the earliest scribbles through to the artistic activities of the adult and later years. A significant part of this art history is drawing. Even without any art classes during the formative early school years and through high school, drawing is an activity that each child does regardless of instruction or guidance.

Each person's art history and developmental sequence is unique and very important in understanding where one stands with art as an adult. People can be very sensitive and this needs to be approached with care. The process of development in drawing is a gradual focusing—from seeing the world in soft, dreamy tones and shapes to seeing it in depth and perspective, light and dark. We will explore the four distinct stages: the preschooler, the elementary student, the high school adolescent and the adult.

The preschooler

A very young child loves to "scribble" and will happily make her mark on all kinds of surfaces! It is not long before the dynamic scribbles begin to take on circular shapes, which can stand for all kinds of forms, from a fish to a person. The picture is what the

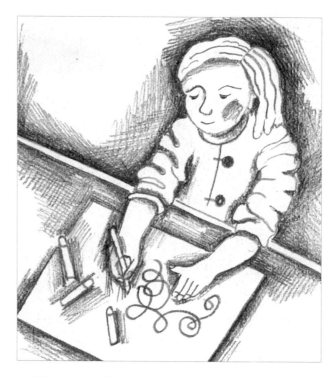

child says it is. Slowly on, the picture becomes more differentiated. Recognizable shapes begin to appear, along with an increasing developing awareness of the world. Legs, arms and even details in clothing can be seen in the drawings of four-year-olds.

Around the age of five, children's drawings begin to tell stories, the different elements begin to be recognizable and a certain degree of order starts to appear. Many studies have been undertaken to interpret children's drawings. In her book, *Understanding Children's Drawings,* Michaela Strauss correlates the stages of children's drawings to the different stages of civilization, and she wonders whether children's drawings are impressions of "footprints" on the path to adulthood.

The elementary grades

Gradually the drawings begin to have a resemblance to a landscape as well as figures and animals, with the ground at the bottom, the sky at top and a house and tree in between. The child develops spatial orientation on the page and begins to show a sense for above and below, forwards and backwards.

A six- to eight-year-old will draw a picture of herself as she feels inwardly—the drawing is an expression of inner feelings and sensations. Often the drawings have great charm and are of special interest to the kindergarten and early grades teachers. These drawings can profoundly reveal a child's developmental stage and whether she is ready for first grade. As part of the first grade readiness assessment, children can be asked to draw a "Person, House, Tree" picture, which can reveal whether the child has spatial awareness of ground and sky and a sense of herself in the world (see Audrey McAllen, *The Extra Lesson,* 1992, p. 98).

For the child, it is an inner world of truth in which she is fully immersed and completely at one with. It is as though at first the gaze is turned entirely inwards. Then slowly there is a looking through the windows, and finally there is a movement through the door into the outer surroundings. The changing of this inner world to the outer world comes gradually between the years of seven and nine. The child's consciousness now comes forth from out of a "dream condition" and in the course of its development it turns actively towards the world outside. – Audrey McAllen

Imagination

The drawings of the seven-year-old well up from the imagination in a way that is unique and lasts only a short time in the overall development of drawing. For instance, an animal will be portrayed as the child feels and senses it and may bear little resemblance to outward reality and perception. There is innocence and a childlike quality about these drawings that show the child is still in the stage of development before the intellect begins to awaken.

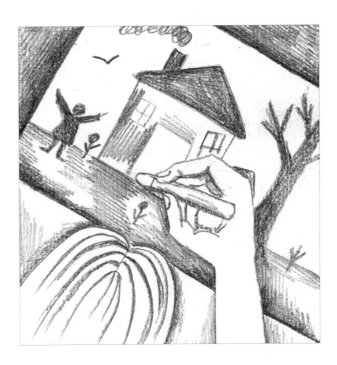

The separation

By about the age of nine or ten, the child begins to see the world as separate from herself, and this is very strongly reflected in her drawings. The nine-year-old becomes very concerned with how things "look" and can become self-critical as well as critical of other children. This passion for realism can become overpowering for the child, and this stage of each person's development is crucial to his or her future success and enjoyment of drawing in later life. More often than not, it is during this stage that children have a negative experience of their own drawing, artistic ability and skills, which blocks the way for them to ever pick up a pencil again.

A girl came up to me in grade two and said, "Why do your people's arms come from the hips?" Apparently I didn't know the placement of arms back then. This comment really frustrated me and put a bit of discouragement into my head.
– E.D., class of 2011

It is of great importance for the teacher to keep an eye out for how students interact as regards their drawing skills.

39

The nine-year-old

Nine-year-olds love drawing and want to draw, but often what they perceive cannot be put down on paper in a way that satisfies them. The child often does not have the skills yet to render an anatomically correct human being or animal. Also, at this age the beginnings of seeing perspective come about and the awareness of far and near, round and flat, light and dark are dawning. In the third grade drawing left top, the nine-year-old drew the house with a side view as well as a shadow on the ground from the tree trunk. This awareness is the exception rather than the norm as shown by the drawing that follows, where the house is portrayed more typically with the front facing forward.

The thirteen- or fourteen-year-old

Around the age of thirteen or fourteen, the young adolescent is ready to explore full perspective and "sculptural" three-dimensional drawing. Houses are often portrayed with front and side views, although in some cases still rendered quite simply. Students are ready to be given exercises in light and dark and in perspective, and to learn how to create the effect of distance in a landscape. At this age students can benefit from studying great artists like Dürer and learning from copying.

The high school years

The high school years can be a wonderful culmination and honing of increased skills and development of styles of expression. Along with an increasing ability to place on the paper what is

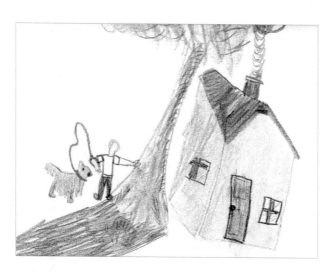

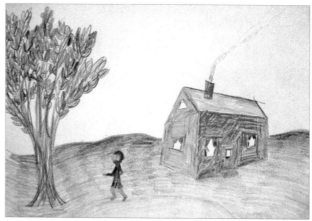

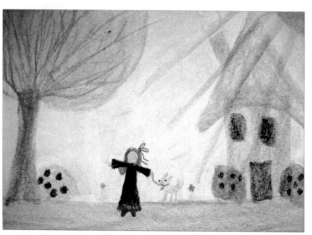

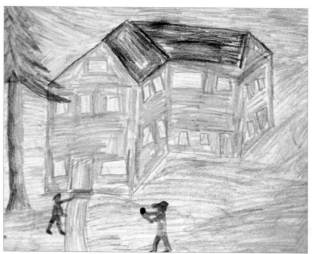

perceived as reality, students now have an ability to understand what "abstract" means and can make the step beyond what looks "real."

Drawing becomes much more specialized, as lessons in human figure and still life drawing play an important part in the development of the students' artistic ability. They are now able to create their own likeness in a self-portrait, such as this example from a freshman.

In Waldorf high schools, students have main blocks of study that last for about three weeks, much like the students in Waldorf elementary grades. Students are expected to make their own main lesson books from what they learn about the subject from the teacher and from their own research. They are encouraged to illustrate their books with color and black and white illustrations. Portraits of historic figures and demonstrations of science experiments are some examples. Drawing in the high school can be a rich experience for students.

Adult years

Not many people draw as adults. For many adults, drawing is something they leave behind in school during those crucial middle school years, never to be taken up again. Sketching while traveling is largely taken over by photography. Illustrating books is mostly left up to artists and illustrators. Adults enjoy watching their children draw and receiving and collecting their children's art. In general, most adults are shy, if not critical, of their own skills and, in addition, may harbor a dormant frustration from the early years.

A possibility of new beginnings

Many adults do not realize that a new beginning is possible—they too can learn to draw. There are wonderful books that take the adult step by step towards real success. *Drawing on the Right Side of the Brain* by Betty Edwards, *The Natural Way to Draw* by Kimon Nicolaïdes, and *Drawing from the Book of Nature* (see "Drawing with a breathing tone") by Dennis Klocek are some examples of books that can be studied. There are different approaches to be discovered and learned, each one having its

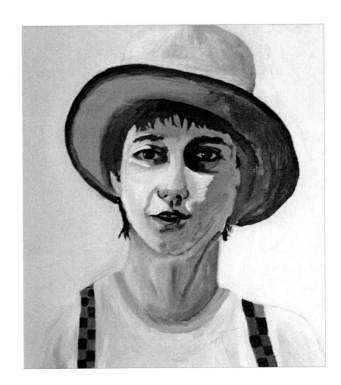

particular and special merit. Every adult as a unique human being can find the way back to exploring and discovering his or her own unique talents—whether in drawing, painting or sculpture, ceramics, weaving or knitting.

By taking up drawing in a renewed way, adults can discover that they have had a talent for drawing that was hidden all those years when they thought they were incapable. Art can be "beautiful" to the creator and beholder without being a precise, naturalistic and accurate representation of the visible world around us.

Age-appropriate drawing

The knowledge—that what is known about Art—is common property.
It is in many books. What the teacher can do is to point out the road that leads to
accomplishment and try to persuade her students to take that road.

- Kimon Nicolaïdes

In the early years when children are beginning to learn to draw, it is important for the teacher to draw with them according to their maturity and ability. This is a critical part of ensuring success in drawing because it is easy for students to become discouraged if the task before them looks too difficult.

This also applies in later years, especially around sixth grade and onwards. Students become very self-conscious about their work. They can become so discouraged that they lose all self-confidence and shut down. Therefore, in all the grades, it is best to draw appropriately according to the age level. This can be a hard proposition for the teacher who is talented artistically and is used to drawing with expertise. However, it can come as a relief to the teacher who is just starting out, does not have much artistic talent and can learn drawing skills along with the children.

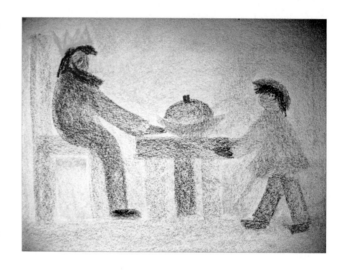

I always had a hard time drawing realistic animals with the right proportions.

- L.Ho., class of 2011

The first three years

A teacher needs to observe carefully what children are capable of drawing. Most children come into first grade having had no formal drawing instruction, which is very appropriate. They have been allowed to draw freely up to this point and are now ready to learn to draw.

Beginning at a very simple level to get them started on their journey, the teacher can demonstrate in front of them and they will follow, especially if it is done imaginatively and connected to a story they have heard.

From the ground up

In the early years the best way to begin a drawing is to start with the earth below. The earth is shown flat without a background of hills or mountains. The figures and shapes positioned on the earth should be large and shown either from a frontal or a side view.

Animals are hard to draw, and drawing a figure or animal at an angle is too challenging for young children. Drawing a frontal view of an animal shape is difficult and can be confusing. Any foreshortening is out of reach for most elementary students, even in the middle school years. To make them easy to draw, they should always be drawn from a side view.

Figures, houses and trees

It is fascinating to observe how a child matures over the years in her ability to draw the main three ingredients of a drawing: a person, a house and a tree. The figures, houses and trees go on a journey of development all the way through high school.

In the early years a tree will have a trunk and a big ball of green on top. Beginning in grade one students can be shown how to articulate the branches and leaves, from a very first simple tree to a more complex shape in the middle school. Start with the roots and work upwards through the trunk and out into the branches, just as a plant grows—from the base.

The human being can be depicted full-bodied in its entirety, from head to feet, before adding the clothes. This aids the child in body geography awareness as you work down from the head along the neck, over the shoulders down the trunk right down to the feet. Animals can also begin at the head and be worked downwards along the neck, the torso, the legs and the tail.

Light and dark

Young children can see shadows and have fun creating animal shapes with their hands in front of a light. Yet they are not, for the most part, intellectually aware of how shadows are created. They are also unable to make something they draw look rounded and three-dimensional with the aid of darker tones.

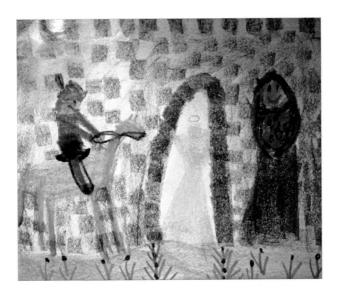

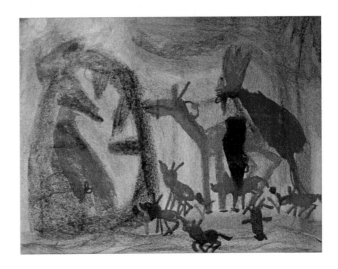

They tend to draw their figures flat with even tones. The ability to show three-dimensionality in forms and shapes needs to wait until the middle school.

Proportions

Children up to the age of ten or eleven are unaware of the proportions of the human figure, as well as proportional relationships between objects, such as a person and a house. Children up to that age represent the environment around them subjectively, according to what is important to them and what the drawing is meant to convey.

Viktor Lowenfeld, in *Creative and Mental Growth*, states how important it is not to judge the child.

We therefore have no right to speak of "false proportions," since such a judgment is determined by an adult visual attitude, the attitude of objectively representing the environment. On the contrary, it is only when we understand the reasons for these apparent disproportions that we are able to penetrate into the true basis of creativeness.

Since the young child is unaware of drawing objects disproportionately to their size in relation to other objects, it is best for the teacher not to correct the students. Their sense of proportion will develop naturally and gradually.

In *Art and Visual Perception*, Rudolf Arnheim states that "visual form moves from stage to stage lawfully, and each stage has its own justification, its own capacities for expression, its own beauty. Since these early stages depend on one another and lay the foundation for any mature achievement, they must be worked through unhurriedly. This is true not only for children but for developing artists."

Perspective

It is the same with perspective. Most students begin to see perspective only in the middle school years. It is best to introduce it slowly and gradually. Even after working with perspective for three weeks in seventh grade, students are challenged to master it even on a simple level.

For example, in third grade, when drawing a farm, there are so many elements to include and the children are becoming more conscious and mature. Hills can be introduced in the background and a garden placed in the foreground. (If the students live in flat terrain, the teacher can always talk about a wonderful place such as New Hampshire where the cows graze on gently undulating fields with stonewalls surrounding them.)

Ages 10 to 14

As the students mature, so will their drawing ability. They will begin to be able to observe shadows on a tree trunk in a fifth grade botany lesson. They can learn how to draw shadows to make an object look three-dimensional, such as on a cup or teapot (see

"Middle school drawing"). It is important that they are shown how to draw shadows and how to learn to draw objects and buildings in perspective.

Being one step ahead

It is ideal for the teacher to be always one or even two steps ahead of the students, to encourage them onwards on their drawing journey, to give them new heights to reach for. The teacher on an eight-year journey with a class can work on her style and skills and grow along with the students. Being a few steps ahead gives the children a goal to strive for.

Drawing on the board

It is best to keep drawings on the blackboard at the same level of development as that of the students, whether the board drawing is created to depict a particular aspect of the main lesson block or to serve as a guided drawing done in front of the children. Children can easily become overwhelmed by a board drawing that seems too sophisticated for them and that they have difficulties emulating.

Noah's ark

Let's take, for example, a depiction of Noah's ark in third grade. Here are two versions—one simple view from the front (below) and one rendered in perspective (top next page). The simple version is at the ability of the nine-year-old. The alternative is appropriate for seventh grade and up. It would not be suitable for the teacher to draw a side view of a tall ship without some indication of perspective

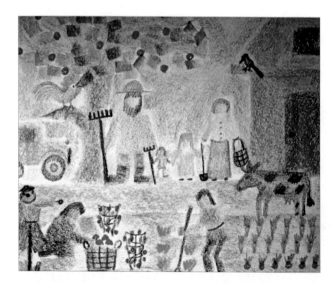

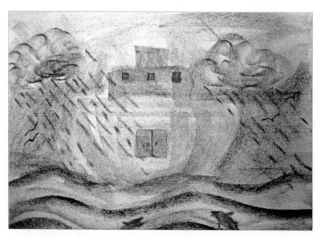

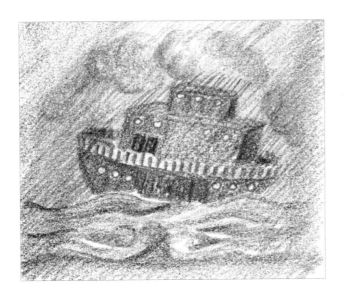

in a seventh grade explorers unit, especially if the perspective unit has already been taught. If the unit is still to come, the teacher can introduce the concept and keep it simple.

Geography

Children love to draw maps. Drawing maps brings a sense of place alive and adds meaning and enjoyment to the learning process.

David Sobel, in his book *Mapmaking with Children,* has done extensive research in mapmaking by children at different stages of development. He saw consistent patterns of development not necessarily dependent on environment and culture. After analyzing many maps drawn by children, he could see

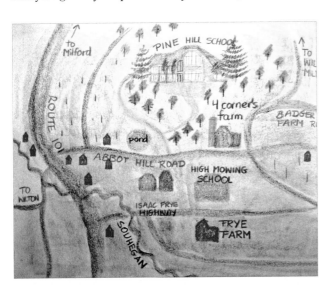

that the vantage point changes according to the child's development. While an 11- to 14-year-old has the ability to gain a sense of distance and perspective, the view of the 7- to 8-year-old is still low to the ground. The map drawing is rich in pictorial content, with houses and trees standing upright along the roads. As the child develops, the angle of the view rises by degrees until finally the map becomes a more abstract view from above. The pictorial content gradually decreases, the map becomes more true to scale, and symbols replace the pictorial.

Advocating a holistic approach

Sobel explains that children need to be given opportunities to draw maps according to their development. An age-appropriate map allows the child to be able to freely express pictorial content and gradually develop the capacity for drawing a more sophisticated bird's eye view:

We do disservice to children when we jump in too quickly at a prematurely abstract level in map reading and mapmaking. The progression of children's mapmaking skills is a microcosm of cognitive development in elementary school.

Going all out in the middle school

By the time the teacher and students reach middle school, drawings can become as sophisticated as the teacher can muster. The aim is to impress the students whenever possible! A fabulous drawing on the board will go a long way, and teachers need all they can get for accolades in the challenging years of middle school.

I gained confidence from every drawing I did. The more practice I got, the more my confidence grew and allowed me to transform into a confident artist. — E.S., class of 2011

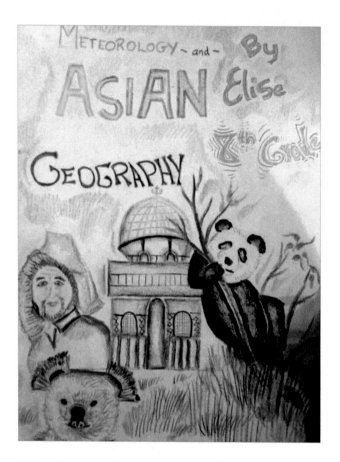

Frequent practice

Many teachers who are new to Waldorf education are also new to the drawing approach, or simply new to drawing. For them it is essential to practice frequently and to at least keep up with the students' pace, or the teacher will be left behind. It is fine for the students to see the teacher's striving, as drawing does not come naturally to every teacher. Frequent practice goes a long way in developing drawing skills—the hand and eye coordination can be trained.

Imagination and imaging are more difficult to practice, but both can also be worked on with effort and determination. Becoming a confident teacher standing up in front of the children and drawing on the board with ease and enjoyment is a wonderful experience.

Why is this all so important?

The overall aim in art education is to foster self-confidence in the student's ability, whether in painting, modeling, drawing or any other form of expression. Fostering this confidence begins in first grade and should continue through high school and beyond. The successful teacher allows the students to develop gradually at their own pace according to their age level and maturity. She demonstrates drawing that they can follow and works with them in a way that makes them feel successful about their work.

This includes giving them freedom of expression within the confines of the lesson. Art education is not so much about the teacher's prowess as it is about the learning student. If you are a fabulous artist and used to demonstrating your formidable skills, teaching in the lower grades asks for restraint and patience. Your time will come in the middle school years when you can show off your skills and enjoy drawing with your individual expertise.

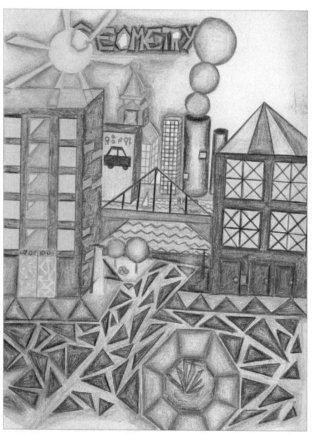

Why drawing in the classroom?

With eye and brain, we only look.
With eye, brain and drawing hand, we are able to truly see.
Drawing is an artistic bridge that connects us to the world.

– Arthur Auer

Many activities that take place in the classroom help students understand the content of the lessons. The activity of drawing can greatly enhance and enrich the learning process. Bringing in and creating visual images can also expedite the learning process for those children who are visual, as opposed to those who are linear learners.

Listening to stories

Listening to stories—from fairy tales in the first grade to the biography of Caesar in the sixth grade— stirs children's imagination and brings the history of humanity alive with meaning. The telling of stories and legends creates inner pictures before the mind's eye of the students. Along with the written word, the visual images bring the pages of their main lesson books to life with color and artistry. A story told one day can be recalled and remembered the next day, followed by the students' writing an essay and

drawing an illustration. Illustrations bring the written words to life. A book without images lacks a sense of life and seems empty. When drawings accompany a text, the work becomes a meaningful whole, where the two worlds of the intellect and art come together. If no pictures accompany the writing, then a decorative border with colors and design brightens the page of words.

Drawing as a balance

Intellectual activity needs a complementary artistic activity as its companion or counterpart. For children, the focused act of careful writing may take a considerable amount of energy and be quite draining of their life forces. Drawing in the classroom brings about a balance between working with the head and heart forces. In addition, children are able to express words on paper in visual form with shapes and images, each in their own unique way.

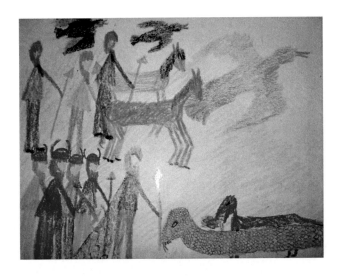

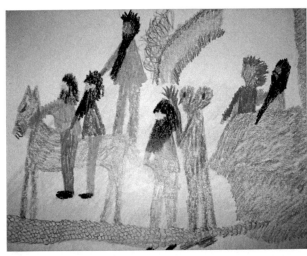

47

Learning about aesthetics

Drawing in the classroom can be one of the activities that helps guide children towards a sense for aesthetics. The beauty of color and form can be found and created through all images brought by words. A picture is worth a thousand words and drawings are stories in themselves—they do not necessarily need to be accompanied by words. Rarely would we say, "This painting needs a page or two of writing to balance it out" (unless we cannot figure out what the painting is meant to convey—but even then it may be left to remain a mystery). Drawing in the classroom can give the students the early foundation they need for an actual drawing class in the middle school and beyond.

Laying the foundation

Drawing lays the foundation for understanding spatial relationships of above and below, left and right, before and behind. It lays the foundation for learning the composition of a picture, how to arrange the numerous elements of the picture into a balanced whole. If drawing in the classroom is done frequently, it stands a chance to remain a natural activity. The process of learning becomes integrated—drawing, as well as other artistic activities, becomes a natural part of learning.

Drawing as a tool for learning

Drawing is a tool for learning about the world. For example, a student watches a physics experiment and later writes about it. What better way to help the learning process than to create a picture of it to accompany the words? Words that describe an event are sometimes not easily understood. By contrast, as soon as a picture appears, the description is more readily accessible, especially to the visual learner.

Learning to appreciate quality work

Care over artistic work is something that needs to be learned by students working in the classroom. Learning what it means to create a beautiful picture and to take care of its overall look is an invaluable learning process for life. Children tend to rush the end of a drawing and need encouragement at times to slow down and work carefully right up to the end.

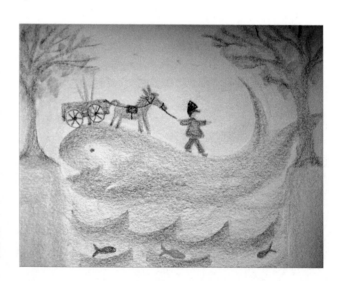

Drawing as seeing

Drawing a picture along with the text enhances a lesson when a class is studying animals and learning about them in their natural environments. Drawing animals helps students to see the animal in a new way and makes them look at the shapes and forms and gestures in a way that is just not possible with mere words.

When visiting a farm, having third graders draw the animals is a wonderful complement to the daily chores of feeding and grooming. The students can touch the animals with their hands, feel the hard spine of the cow and the softness of the hide. The experience is further enhanced by sitting down and writing and drawing in their notebooks. (However, this should not be a specific assignment to copy the animal, but rather a free choice of drawing to enhance their journaling.)

Drawing in nature in the older grades is another way of bringing the many different shapes and forms alive to the students. Flowers can be transformed into linear form drawings, and the shapes of tree trunks and mushrooms can become some of the first lessons in roundness and three-dimensional form.

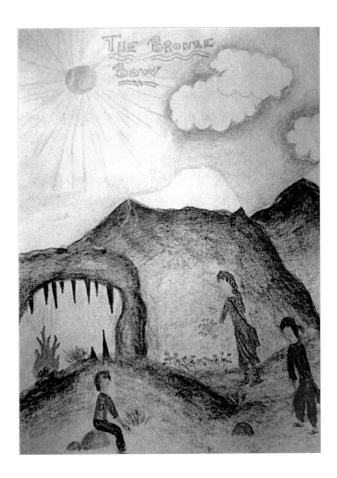

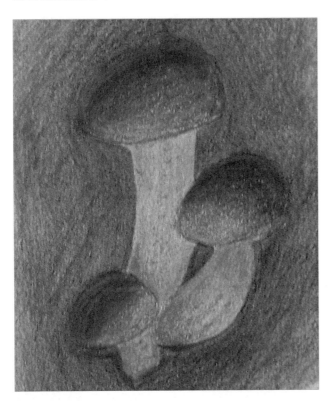

Seeing is knowing

In order to know and understand, we must learn to see. This is a crucial aspect for learning. Drawing challenges often arise because many of us never look and observe properly. When we try to draw something, we cannot remember whether a leg goes this way or that, how long or short the legs should be, and so on. We have looked, but we have not truly seen. Seeing and drawing work as aids to learning and understanding the world around us.

Drawing made me look closer at my surroundings. My observation skills were sharpened. – E.D., class of 2011

Enhancement of the sense of touch

Drawing combines and enhances the use of several senses—the sense of sight, the sense of movement (in the arm and hand) and the sense of touch. Touch is mentioned here not in the sense of

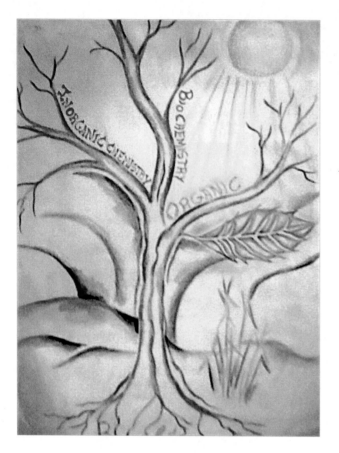

Many aspects to drawing

There are many different techniques and approaches to drawing in the classroom. Learning about and understanding perspective can enhance a student's spatial imagination and aid in making sense of what the eye perceives. Discovering how to create a three-dimensional form from a flat form can help students understand the world around them. Learning how light and shadow play an integral part in making it possible for us to distinguish whether something is three- or two-dimensional is crucial in the process of learning to see.

Using the hands in drawing, modeling and other arts means not only that the eyes are guiding and assisting our hands, but also that the hands are teaching the eyes to really look actively. The hands are organs of our will to action. They are our "doers" who transform the world. By working in mutual cooperation with the eyes, the hands bring will power into our eyes and change passive seeing into real looking at things.

– Arthur Auer

Overcoming obstacles

When drawing after the age of nine, and especially later as adults, children often feel inhibited by those around them. They feel a lack of confidence in their skills when they compare their work with that of others or they perceive that their work is not satisfactory.

Everyone as an artist

Many adults have been brought up with coloring books and cartoon-type line drawings and have not had basic guidance in three-dimensional drawing. They feel inadequate and lack confidence, with the sure knowledge and belief that they are not artists and never will be. Yet everyone has the artist in them—and this artist needs to find the time and place to be discovered and nurtured.

what it might normally mean—a physical touch. Our eyes "touch" all that we see, and the more the eye touches, the more conscious the touching becomes. What the eye sees has become a conscious process of perceiving. We can all dream away into a landscape and visually enjoy its colors, shapes and hues, and really not consciously understand what we perceive in front of us.

Gradual focus

This seeing, knowing, and understanding is a gradual process of focusing for the young child in the classroom. This gradual process unfolds from the dreamy young student in the early preschool years to the awakening intellect in the middle school. There are very important aspects to this gradual focusing, and how this development can be enhanced and guided at different age levels in the classroom. Much of the success of the students' sense of their own drawing capacity and self-confidence depends on this development through the elementary grades.

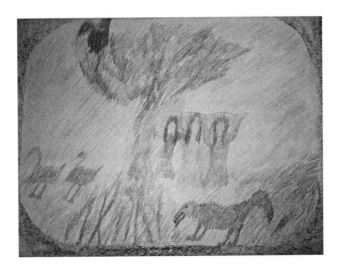

The chapter on "Drawing at different age levels" mentions different approaches for exploring the art of drawing as an adult—free from the tyranny of the 11-year-old's passion for realism. This passion for realism can be so great that it is often the underlying reason young people give up drawing. They remain stuck in this phase, never to reach and develop beyond it.

Drawing phobias

The middle school years are a time of great sensitivity for the adolescent, and drawing can become an insurmountable challenge. Students can develop phobias about drawing that are hard to overcome. They can become fixed in their opinion of themselves as being incapable. In addition, some students may have had the misfortune of having their artwork criticized by peers or, even worse, by their teacher. Something akin to an artistic meltdown can occur and becomes strongly embedded in the psyche.

Adults can suffer for years

In the groups I have taught during my many years of teaching classroom drawing to teacher trainees, there were significant numbers of adults who had experiences like this and had suffered for years. Their teachers in the elementary grades told them that they were no good at drawing and that they should give it up and focus on other subjects they were better at. These students were unable to have a good experience in drawing. This can leave a lifetime scar.

Drawing as part of teaching

In Waldorf schools, students in the elementary grades create their own books documenting the subject content of each block. The teacher often creates her own main lesson book, to refer to or to show as an example. The teacher, especially in the younger grades, draws with the children.

In the older grades, students are more apt to draw on their own with less guidance from the teacher. The teacher will draw some aspect relating to the daily lesson on the blackboard as, for example, an idea for a title page.

The student training to become a teacher in the Waldorf classroom is faced with a new challenge—drawing with the children. For some teachers who have developed their drawing skills beyond the 11-year-old stage, this poses no problem and can be one of the joys of teaching. Their challenge as mentioned earlier is to adjust the level of their drawing to the appropriate age level of the children's drawing and wait to show their artistry in all its glory in the middle school years.

Facing the new challenge

Other teachers find themselves in a real dilemma and wonder how they are going to be able to meet the challenges of drawing. They can become anxious regarding their drawing ability, especially in the middle school years. They worry about how they are going to help the children who are going to need assistance.

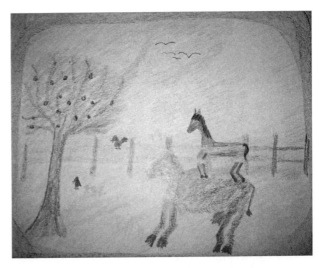

Breaking through the barriers

Taking up drawing in a renewed way can ease a teacher's anxieties, and there can even be a breakthrough—a revelation. Adults can discover that they can cast aside their concerns and begin a new journey. They can also discover that they have their own, unique style. This style may not be obvious at first, but gradually they can become familiar with their own work and begin to gain confidence.

Rediscovering artistry

In the beginning elementary grades, drawing with children is a wonderful way for adults to rediscover their artistry. Beginning with simple drawings, drawn in a painterly way with broad strokes, the new discovery can be an exciting experience. A drawing does not have to be sophisticated in order for it to be "good" art worth looking at. Drawing on a simple level can be acceptable for adults. Drawing together with children can provide a foundation for the adult—an initial stepping-stone for further development.

Confidence will grow from knowing that the teacher is able to produce something that is beautiful to behold, not just to others but also to herself. Confidence will build in knowing that, yes, she too can draw with the children and, most important, in front of the children.

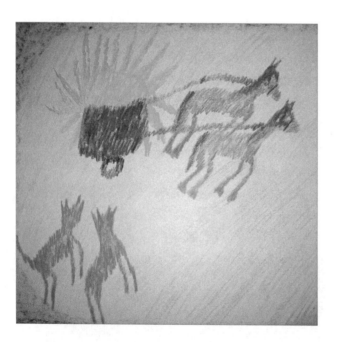

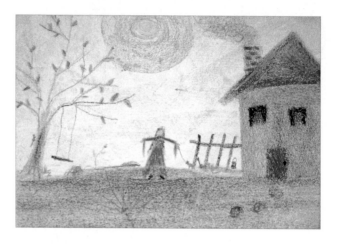

Guiding children

Through practice, the teacher will become familiar with drawing and gain confidence in being able to guide the children. The ability of the teacher to help students with their drawings will in turn help to break the cycle of drawing phobias.

Children often have trouble with drawing animal forms. They love animals and are very keen to draw them. But when they draw them, especially at the ages between eight and ten, they feel that the animals must be satisfying to look at, not only to themselves but also to others. Exclamations such as *"But I don't want mine going up on the bulletin board!" "This wolf looks more like a duck! I hate it; I want to start all over again!"* are examples of the alarm a child can experience. It is an immeasurable gift to the child if the teacher can meet the concern the child feels and guide him towards a more successful outcome.

A gentle approach

Children tend to push down hard with pencils. Drawing a shape or form with broad strokes that give a tone or color can be adjusted if they are initially applied gently. By teaching them to draw lightly, there is a better chance that the children can adjust their drawings to satisfy their quest for realism. Modeling animals in clay or beeswax or other modeling material helps in learning to see and understand the three-dimensional world.

The task of the teacher

It is the task of the teacher to encourage and nurture the potential artist in each child as he or she grows and develops. In turn, it is the task of the teacher to develop her own capacities and abilities so that she can endeavor to help the young child whenever possible.

The teacher's artistic ability can be developed gradually, with patience and practice. Sometimes teachers have to start from the basics and work up to more complex drawings. It is best that they shed the negative experiences they have had in the past and move forward.

Success and enjoyment

The satisfaction of making and completing a beautiful drawing or an entire book is invaluable for both the student and the teacher. The teacher needs to have a confidence and enthusiasm that she shares with the students on their journey of artistry. Working on her skills with which to guide the children will find its rewards in the classroom.

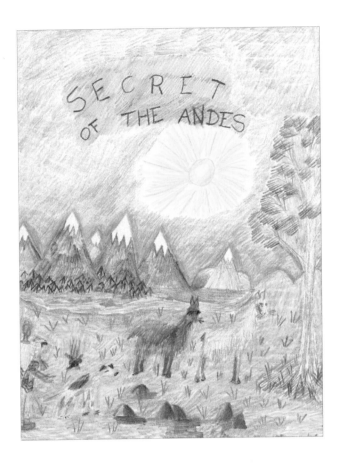

When I entered teacher training I could not draw. Everyone else could draw better than I could, and worse—it was so easy for them! All my life I have struggled with this, finally giving in and saying, "So what? I'll never be an artist."
In preparation for becoming a teacher, I was once again faced with this little demon.
Now here I am three years later with a class going into third grade. My students produce beautiful drawings that fill their pages. And I feel confident in guiding them as well. I know I am not incredibly skilled. But now I am an artist.

- Jennifer Miller, Class Teacher, N.H.

Drawing in the main lesson books

Who is man, the artist? He is the unspoiled core of everyman, before he is choked by schooling, training, conditioning until the artist within shrivels up and is forgotten.
And yet, that core is never destroyed completely. At times it responds to nature, to beauty, to life, suddenly aware again of being in the presence of a Mystery that baffles understanding.

– Frederick Franck

Main lesson books are a unique and important part of the Waldorf classroom and curriculum. Most of what the students have learned is documented in these books. The books are composed entirely by the students and reflect their hard work during the course of their education, from first through twelfth grade. They are a source of pride and accomplishment, much like a portfolio.

The format

The format of main lesson book drawings changes through the grades. Generally, as the children become older, the drawings become smaller. In the older grades there is less time to draw as the academic work becomes progressively more intensive and time-consuming. Increased time spent on writing summaries of the material presented the day before is an example.

The size of the main lesson book drawings changes from full-page drawing in the first to fourth grade to partial-page drawing in fifth through eighth grade. The drawings accompany the text on the same page, rather than the text appearing on the opposite page of the writing.

As the children get older, both the writing and the drawings become more condensed and smaller in format, and the writing increases quantitatively. The writing examples shown here indicate how the size and content of the writing changes through the years. In the first three grades, the children copy what is written on the blackboard. Then by fourth grade students are beginning to write their own essays from the lesson presentations.

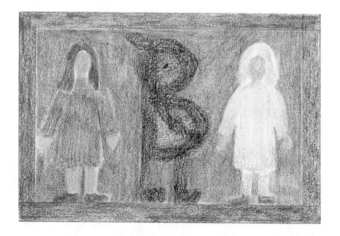

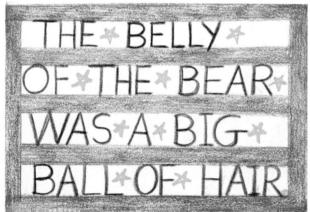

Creating the main lesson book

It is recommended that the teacher create her own main lesson books in preparation for teaching all the blocks. In my experience over the years, in first through eighth grade, this was invaluable in preparing for the lessons. Having a main lesson book prepared and always at hand to follow proved to be the best approach throughout the year. It allowed for a sense of security through the weeks and months, knowing that the material was ready to be easily accessed, and alleviated much of the daily pressures of classroom teaching and all that it entails. Looking back at what I actually did with the class relative to what I had prepared, I was able to follow my initial plan for the most part through careful and realistic planning of the blocks (on a daily basis) according to the school calendar.

Finding the time

Preparing a whole year's worth of lessons is a daunting task. It takes a considerable amount of time and the ability to look ahead, and it involves gathering the necessary research material for the blocks. There are many experienced teachers to consult and to learn from, especially when starting out. Beginning teachers can be guided in their block outlines and lesson material by more experienced teachers. There are also many great resources available on class teaching subjects that can help orient the new teacher.

After a few years' experience in the classroom, a teacher develops a good idea of the projects to go along with the lessons, as well as realistic expectations and pace, given the hours available in any given school day. It is always better to prepare too much rather than too little.

Organizational skills

Good organizational skills and being proactive are essential ingredients in maximizing preparation time. With research material at hand, writing up the material takes focused effort, while preparing drawings is an activity that can be done separately. Having materials at hand, you can find and make time, for instance, during faculty meetings when the participation is mostly through active listening.

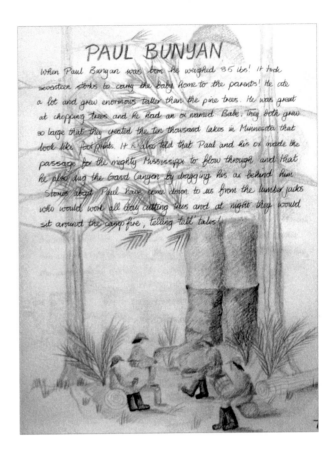

One such example of an economical use of time is professional days before and at the end of the school year. During these days of much listening, with pencils on hand, many of the drawings that have been sketched out can be enhanced and completed. At home, if there are children around, provide them with drawing materials while you work on your book so that they can join in the activity. Alternatively, work on the drawings while you sit next to them, helping them with their homework. I once took my book and pencils along with me on what could have been a long tedious plane ride and accomplished many drawings—and time flew!

How to decide on what to draw

In general, each story or main lesson content has a central theme or character that can be depicted. The illustration accompanying the story or presentation needs to capture the essence of the content. This can be an action taken by one or the other character(s). Since there is only one drawing possible with each story, it needs to convey the most essential aspects.

For example, in the second grade story of Saint Gudwalis, the drawing illustrates the cave with Gudwalis and the student protected by a sandbar created by the fishes.

First grade

Examples of drawings for first grade on the CD include ideas for drawing several consonants and vowels, ideas for number-related drawings, math gnomes, and a series of fairy tales and nature stories.

The children enjoy creating illustrations of the letters. Once they get going they often take pleasure in guessing the letter when they see the suggestive picture. For the consonants it is recommended to find images that imbue action (verbs), such as running for R and jumping for J. The aim is to draw the image as organically and authentically as possible, rather than intellectually contrived. This can be a challenge with some letters, such as X.

Drawing with children

The teacher draws in front of the children, either with chalk on the blackboard, with crayons and paper on an easel, or on paper taped to the board. She positions herself to the side, so that all children can see and follow.

Drawings prepared by the teacher are generally not hung up on the board for all children to copy. Rather, the teacher guides the children through the drawing step by step, without displaying a finished product. This means that the teacher has practiced the drawing at home and sketches it out anew in the classroom in front of the children.

Another possibility is that the teacher brings the sketch into the classroom but keeps it at the side to use or refer to, but without showing it to the children. This is certainly a good back-up plan for any new teacher still working her way towards more self-confidence in drawing. What is most important is that the children experience the teacher's artistry in direct action and then render in their own way what they see. They are not expected to slavishly and exactly copy the teacher's work.

The size of the drawing can be a full page, opposite the writing. During this first year, the drawing can be placed on the left page. The right page is kept blank for writing the sentences later on in the year after the children have learned all their letters and can copy a few sentences from the board. The practice of the corresponding large capital letters can be done on the following page, along with eventual practice of lowercase letters. Four pages are used for each letter: one for the drawing, one for writing the sentences, one for practicing the letter as a large capital and one for practicing capital and lowercase letters. With this format, when the children are ready to write the sentences, the teacher recalls the story with them.

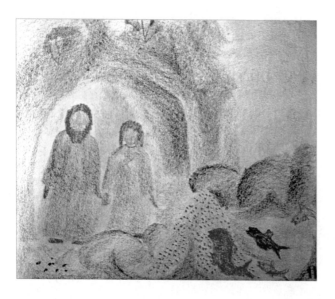

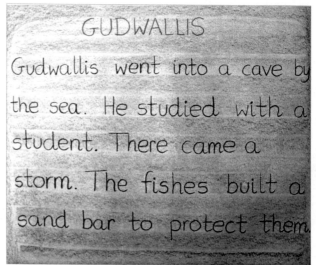

GUDWALLIS

Gudwallis went into a cave by the sea. He studied with a student. There came a storm. The fishes built a sand bar to protect them.

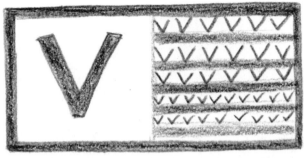

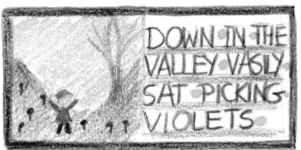

Second grade

In drawings for the second grade diagrammatic elements are added, such as numbers with math gnomes, a number place shelf, nature stories, fables and legends of the saints. The size for the drawings remains basically the same as for grade one, the drawing again accompanying the writing that has now become smaller and contains both uppercase and lowercase letters. Typically the writing page contains three to five sentences, mostly copied from the board.

Keeping things simple

Images are drawn on a basic level appropriate for this age and development. Young children are not yet able to draw images that are angled in complicated ways. The aim at all times is to encourage success, to build their confidence. Presenting them with complex, angled drawings can create frustration and potentially cause needless anxiety. Basic drawing is challenging enough as it is at times, for both the child and the teacher. The teacher really needs to place herself in the child's position and pave the way for success. So show either a full side or frontal view of animals, human beings, plants and buildings.

This does not mean that the children or the teacher should not include interesting details. Children love to add their own details, such as birds' nests and squirrels. Allow the children to have some freedom in the colors they choose, so as to cultivate free expression.

Third grade

The third grade curriculum contains Old Testament stories and Native American stories as well as house building, farming and measurement. Some drawings can be part pictorial and part diagram, such as the example of the compost pile or the illustration for measuring liquid volume.

Showing liquid volume pictorially is very helpful to understanding the concept. Seeing the

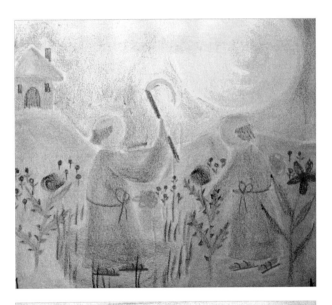

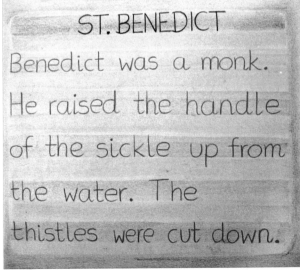

relationships between the size of a liquid gallon and how four quarts fit into a gallon and how two pints fit into each quart, and so on, makes for improved comprehension and memory. The same principle can be applied to linear measurement and weight. Pictorially showing a scale for balance and how a ruler relates to a human foot is helpful.

Third graders can continue to use block and stick crayons for another year to perfect their surface tone technique. Basically, they are not yet ready to create consistent surface tone with a sharp point or even a soft pencil. If pencils are introduced too early, much of the surface tones will be scratchy and have a scribbled look.

Becoming more independent

This is the turning point of the golden age of innocence in drawing. Children who felt themselves at one with the world and were fully able to immerse themselves in drawing without worrying about realism now experience the nine-year-old change. They begin to see themselves as separate from the world and this has an effect on their drawing. They become more questioning and concerned about realism. They also become more independent and many are able to draw on their own without any guidance or help. They will generally keep to the standard set by the teacher, yet they often need reminders to be careful when drawing large surface areas such as the sky.

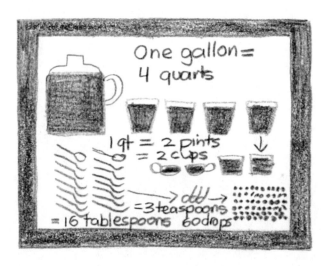

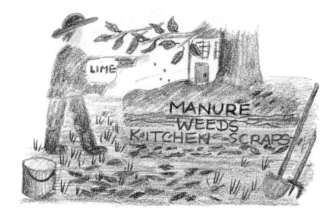

Children at this age tend to spend a lot of time on the action parts of their drawings and then finish up in a hurry once their main interest is satisfied. Some have not yet sufficiently developed their own pictorial images and continue to need considerable guidance. For them the guidance of the teacher is still crucial.

Fourth grade

Fourth grade includes drawings about Norse myths, fractions, local geography, and the human being and animal. Ideas for main lesson book illustrations for this grade are shown as done primarily in diagonal shading and in colored pencils. Also included are sample pages of writing.

Halfway through the elementary grades, most, if not all, of the children are able to draw independently without much, if any, guidance. The teacher can give suggestions as to what to draw, and for many that is sufficient to get them started. Some children will need more than suggestions and perhaps a sketch by the teacher to give them a starting point.

It is highly recommended to give the children plenty of opportunities to create their own drawings and to allow them to have ideas of their own as to what to draw. Sometimes children want to include two scenes rather than just one and will create two smaller drawings. Occasionally allow the children to divide the page into four with a border separating the four spaces, which allows for four little scenes pertaining to the story.

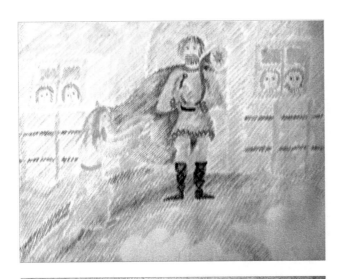

HEIMDALL, THE WATCHMAN
One of Odin's sons was Heimdall. He was a watchman for the Aesir. He was an excellent watchman for his clear blue eyes could see all the way to the end of the world. He also had very sharp ears and could hear every thing. He hardly slept. Mostly he stood at the bottom of the rainbow bridge making sure no one could sneak into Asgard.
Odin had given him a horn to blow whenever he saw danger approaching. He named it Gjallarhorn, It was so loud that it could be heard all over the world. He let in Gullveig, from the Vanir gods, the far away world of the singing winds. She was bewitchingly beautiful, but she was a witch.

The use of borders

As the students move up through the grades, academic work becomes increasingly intellectually absorbing and challenging, and much time is spent on achieving good writing skills in composing essays, reports and summaries. Less time is available for drawing. Elaborate borders are aesthetically pleasing but time-consuming. A general rule might be that students work on borders only if they have completed all their assignments. If borders are marked out in pencil and time does not allow for completing them in an illustrative way, the borders can be colored in with beeswax blocks.

The size of the drawing shrinks to a smaller format—from 14" x 17" to 11" x 14". For fourth grade we still used the book horizontally, with a full page of writing on one side and a drawing on the other.

Drawing maps

In fourth grade large area surfaces for maps are perhaps best done with blocks rather than drawing with the slant line technique. While learning about local geography in fourth grade, children should begin with drawing maps in a simple, non-sophisticated manner that includes pictorial content of houses, churches and trees that are standing upright. A state map of New Hampshire, or whatever state or province is your home, can include the state or provincial bird, tree and flower to augment the learning experience. Maps in fifth grade become more abstract, with illustrations becoming more symbolic rather than pictorial.

Fifth grade

Fifth grade curriculum includes Ancient history of India, Persia, Mesopotamia, Egypt and Greece, as well as botany and North American geography. It is possible to stay with the larger size of 11" x 14" as used in fourth grade. The main lesson book size commonly used for the middle school years is 9" x 12", and vertical rather than horizontal.

In the fifth grade a change can be made from full-size page drawings to pages that combine writing and illustration. Rather than being placed on its own on the opposite page, the drawing now accompanies the writing in an integrated manner. This provides opportunity for variety, as well as for smaller drawings that do not take as much time.

All the examples for fifth grade show pages with illustrations included as part of the page. The students write the content and then illustrate the page along the bottom under the writing, or they leave a space for their illustration embedded in the writing.

Depending on the thickness of the paper used, writing and drawing leave impressions, especially if the students write with fountain pens. The ink can bleed through to the back side. Leave each left page blank and use only the right-hand pages.

The size of the writing and headings

Fountain pens are often introduced in fifth grade. Students compose most of the writing in the books. A teacher may give a dictation once per week, and occasionally have the children copy from the board. Headings for each page can continue to be done with colored pencils, larger and in capitals to set the headings off from the main writing. The headings can be shaded around or embellished in various ways.

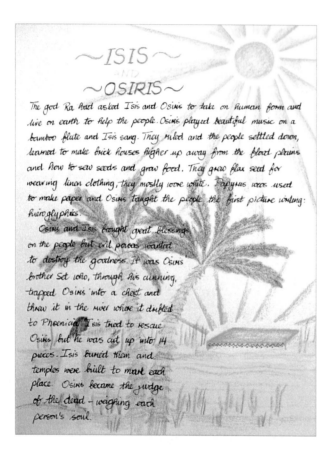

Book illustrations

Students in fifth grade are increasingly capable of making lovely and careful drawings. They are steadily learning about proportions and can begin to have a sense of perspective and shadows. Transitioning from the slant line technique to what is generally termed "shading" with colored pencils can be a smooth process. Drawing with complex angles is still mostly unattainable at this stage, for many even up to high school (and even in high school and beyond). Frontal views and side profiles are still recommended. The illustrations can come right up to the text; on some pages it can go through behind the writing. It will be necessary to give frequent reminders to go easy on the pencils so that the writing does not get too covered over and become illegible.

If fountain pens are used, this is usually not a problem. It is important to stress that the writing must come first as it is not possible to write satisfactorily with pen over pencil drawings.

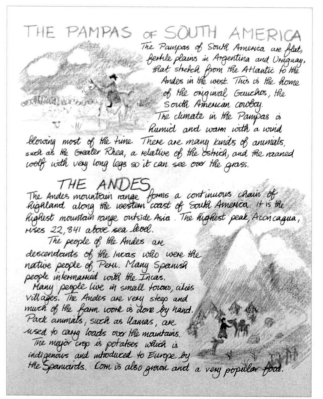

The middle school years

In the sixth grade Roman and medieval history are dominant themes, and physics is taught for the first time as a block. Geography can cover South America. Astronomy and mineralogy are also introduced. Students' illustrations can enhance their understanding of science experiments. The drawings can be positioned right along with the writing, sometimes as many as three drawings per page, depending on how the writing is organized.

Seventh grade main lessons often cover African and European geography, the Renaissance, perspective, physiology, physics and chemistry, and creative writing. Eighth grade blocks cover Asian and world geography, anatomy, meteorology, physics and chemistry, and modern history. Drawings become still smaller during these two years since the students' written work is all self-composed and demands more attention and time. Nevertheless time should be spent on making the pages as illustrated and aesthetically pleasing as possible.

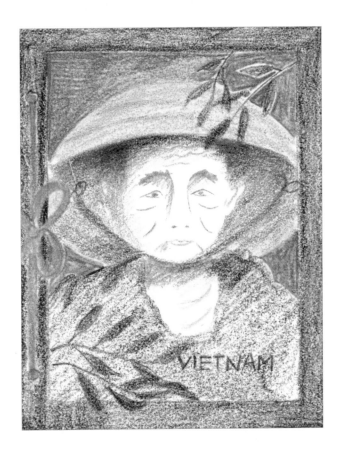

Figure and object drawing

From seventh grade onwards, students should have ample practice at drawing faces and portraits. This aspect of the human being is particularly challenging. Careful guidance in drawing lessons needs to show the proportions of the face as well as the body, so that students can increasingly hone their skills at human figure drawing.

This practice can be greatly enhanced by providing opportunities for students to model in clay. Drawing is two-dimensional on a flat plane, while sculpting is three-dimensional and can increase the students' feeling for form and shape. In addition, students need to practice drawing objects and gain an understanding of shadows.

Book reports and special projects

Drawings can enhance book report covers, and illustrations can be sprinkled throughout the pages of writing pertaining to any subject. In fourth grade, for instance, the animal studies report that can accompany a diorama can be fully illustrated with

a drawing of the animal in its environment on the cover. In eighth grade, when studying biographies of famous people, a portrait done in colored pencils of the person makes for a fabulous front cover.

Binding the pieces

To create a fairly sturdy and substantially bound report, have the students make the illustration for the front cover on a 7" x 10½" piece of paper and paste it (use Yes! Paste) onto a colored piece of 8½" x 11" stock paper, leaving a bit more margin on the left side. Add a back piece of stock paper the same size as the front and punch three holes through the front and back covers using a regular three-hole puncher. Punch the same three holes through the pages of the inside content. Line up the pages and cover to match the holes and sew up the book with colorful ribbon, ending with a small bow. For extra sturdiness, use poster board (cut to size with an Exacto knife) instead of stock paper.

The calendar
A special drawing project for second grade

Second grade is a great year to work on the days of the week and the months of the year, as well as the seasons. Students are learning to write sentences and can apply both their newly acquired language skills and their increasing ability to draw lovely illustrations. Creating a calendar for the new year to come makes for a great holiday gift for the family that lasts all year!

Organization

The calendar project requires great organization and the ability to look ahead in order to time it just right for the end of the semester. The more students in the class, the more complex the task will be for the teacher to pull the calendars all together at the end. This is an inexpensive project, but heavy on the teacher's time and commitment.

Preparation of materials

Second graders need a grid for the month that is prepared for them ahead of time. Make a generic month grid, including the names of the days but not the numbers, with room at the top of the grid for a couple of sentences. (If you have a lot of time for this project, leave the names of the days empty on the grid, so that the students can write them in. Extra practice for spelling the days is beneficial.)

Copy the grid onto 8½" x 11" paper, 12 per student with some extras. Cut drawing paper 8" x 10½" sheets, 12 per student with some extras. The grid and the drawing will fit onto construction paper allowing for a small margin. Make a 13" x 20" folder for each student to contain the drawings and

the monthly grids (before and after they have been pasted on large sheets of construction paper). Keep these folders at the side of their desks or in another suitable storage space. Prepare a calendar of your own, complete with grids and drawings, pasted onto a variety of colored paper.

Introducing the project

Once the students are familiar with the days of the week, months of the year and the number of days per each month, it is time to introduce the project. Make a plan that works for you, your students and your situation. Here's the plan I constructed and how it worked.

During the month of September we practiced sentence writing in upper and lower cases in a language block. I introduced the calendar project during a week in October. I took a whole week and focused on it every morning for an hour to give the children a good start.

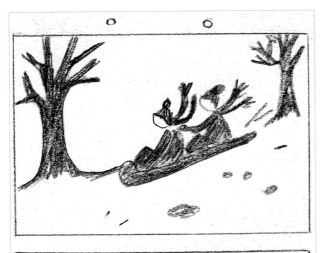

January brings lots of snow
Up and down the hill we go!

We began with drawing together. Then we prepared the first month's grid. Reminding the class at the beginning of how many days are in the month of January, we filled in the numbers, one at a time, very lightly, with graphite pencil, with everyone following and keeping up. I walked around to check all the numbers and gave each individual student the go-ahead to go over the numbers with colored pencil.

Once this was accomplished, the students wrote the sentence for the month in colored pencils, copied from the board. I collected the grids and the drawings at the end of the class, making sure all the students had their initials in a corner. Each student chose their color of construction paper (most chose orange to go with the color of pumpkins).

After the lesson I pasted the grid on the lower half and the drawing on the upper half of the paper for each of the students. In the next lesson I showed them how their first pages looked by hanging them up on the bulletin board for all to admire. I also hung up my October page.

Do all the grids first, then draw

Next we worked on all the grids for the remaining months to include the sentences for each month. Once these were all completed, the students started on the drawings for each month. I hung up the rest of my pages for them to see as examples. Students who needed ideas looked at my drawings—others used their own imagination and were allowed to give it free rein. (This was a great opportunity to give the children freedom to "do their own thing.")

As the project moved along, I tried to keep up with the pasting of the drawings and the grids onto the background construction paper. With the students drawing on their own, my time was freed up so each child could take a turn to come up to the desk and choose the color background for each month that was completed. Allowing the children to draw on

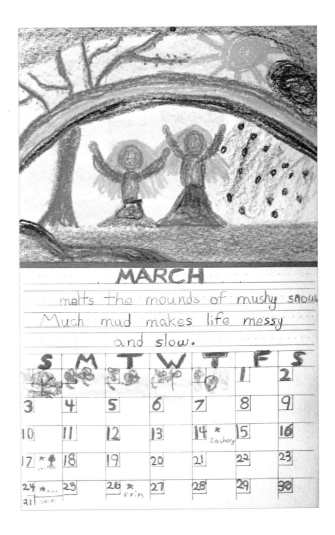

their own also made it possible for students to work at their own pace, making sure the drawings would follow the theme but still be unique.

Initiating your plan

With the leaves turning and the pumpkins ripening, the beginning of October is a great time to start. The students love nothing more than drawing pumpkins and Halloween scenes. They also enjoy making drawings for all the other months; it is natural to begin with January. Delineate your plan to the children so that they can get a sense of how it is all going to work and come together. Give the children plenty of time to work on this project, as all students must have their project completed by the end of the semester. Those who work faster and move ahead can make extra little illustrations in the empty squares where there are no numbered days in the month.

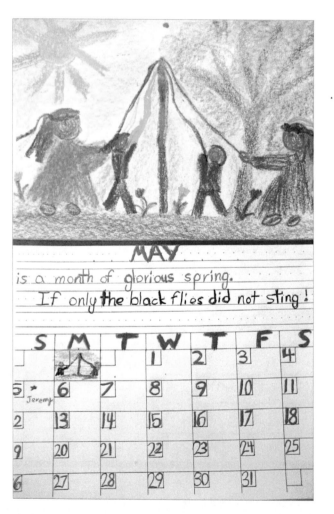

The completed pages

Gradually the completed pages will come "off the press" and begin to accumulate while the number of unfinished drawing pages diminishes. This takes a lot of effort on the teacher's part; careful planning and multitasking will do the trick.

It is best to set up a convenient area for pasting. Using non-toxic Yes! Paste makes for easy cleanup and does the pasting job better than any other glue. (I use the end of a broken ruler to apply the paste onto the paper.) Be sure to cover the whole area of the back of the grid or drawing with a thin layer, carefully placing the drawing in position on the construction paper. Then place a blank piece of paper over the drawing and burnish with the hand. This avoids rubbing back and forth over the actual work, which can smudge the drawing.

Last but not least

Once all the students' work is ready, it is time to write in everyone's birthdays. Do this activity together with all the students, beginning with the month of January. If time allows, final touches can be added to make sure all the pages are completely finished and suitably embellished.

Binding the calendars

Punch two holes at the top of the pages as shown in the illustrations and reinforce the holes with white self-adhesive reinforcement labels. Collect the 12 pages of each student together and, beginning with January in front, thread a finger-knitted string or a ribbon of choice through the two holes and knot the two ends together. The ribbon should hang in a pleasing triangle as shown.

If there is time, it is nice for each student to prepare a calendar cover. The drawing on the front can depict any of the months or show the seasons in a circle or four squares, with the student's name under the year heading.

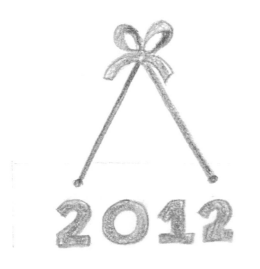

EMILY DANSKO

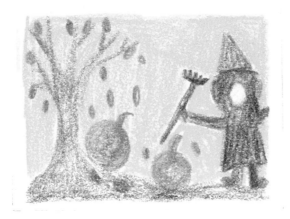

FEBRUARY fills buckets with sap.
Sweet drops of maple fall tap, tap, tap.

MARCH is a month of muddy slush
when melting snow turns into mush.

APRIL begins with a silly fool's day.
Up pop crocuses, colorful and gay.

MAY is a month of glorious spring,
if only the black flies did not sting!

JUNE is full of flowers fair;
bees fly buzzing everywhere.

Swimming is fun in hot JULY.
Fireworks burst all over the sky!

In AUGUST the beach is the best place to be.
We're on vacation, happy and free!

In SEPTEMBER we pick apples from the tree
and head back to school with glee.

OCTOBER colors are orange, yellow and red;
all the plants are going to bed.

NOVEMBER winds blow leaves all around.
They swirl and swirl till they fall to the ground.

DECEMBER is cozy when you sit by the stove.
After being outside you're likely to doze.

Ideas for sentences

If time allows, making up the sentences together with the class is the most fun. Naturally, the sentences pertain to the surrounding geography and state culture.

Children in second grade love to rhyme and you can make it a writing exercise for the class, deciding together which to choose for the calendar. Here are examples of sentences pertaining to "our neck of the woods," as they say, very appropriate for the woodsy terrain and culture of New Hampshire.

JANUARY brings deep snows.
Who has a carrot for a nose?

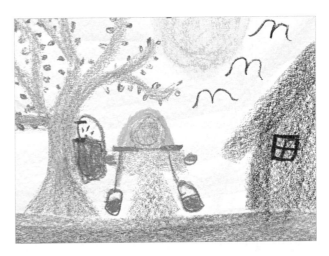

Middle school arts

As students progress into the middle school years,
all subjects build on what has come before,
challenging skill levels in each progressive grade.

– Van James

In the middle school art is given as an individual lesson, a subject on its own. While drawing continues to accompany the main lesson texts in the books, it is important at this point to have a specific time set aside each week for an art lesson. The weekly painting class may have to be shared with drawing and modeling and other projects.

Providing new artistic opportunities for middle school students helps them to expand their horizons and move beyond the basic foundation of their early elementary years. As drawing becomes more challenging, students need to experience a sense of success and accomplishment. This is of crucial importance for their self-confidence in their artistic abilities.

Self-confidence

Students should be encouraged at all times and be given a safe environment in which they can explore new media and new techniques. They can learn to appreciate not only their own work but also that of others. The teacher can act as guide so that all students can feel their efforts are appreciated.

A positive experience in the middle grades will help to keep students artistically alive and thriving through the high school years and beyond. Art in the middle school can lead them towards finding their own mysteriously unique drawing style.

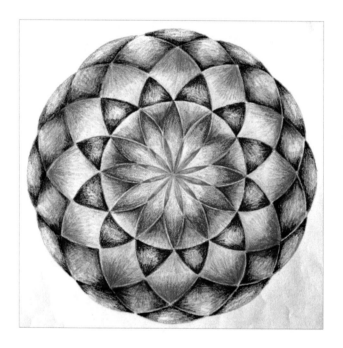

Sixth grade

Geometry

In the early grades, geometry, known as form drawing, is practiced freehand without a ruler or compass. From sixth grade on, geometry becomes increasingly mathematical as students study angles, area, volume of various solids, and the Pythagorean theorem. Students learn to measure carefully and make crisp and clean lines with the ruler, as well as to master the use of the compass by drawing very accurate circles. They can perfect their shading technique with colored pencils and create truly stunning designs with intersecting circles and other geometric shapes and forms.

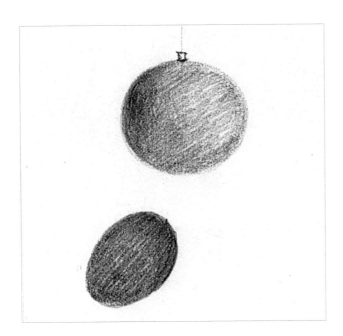

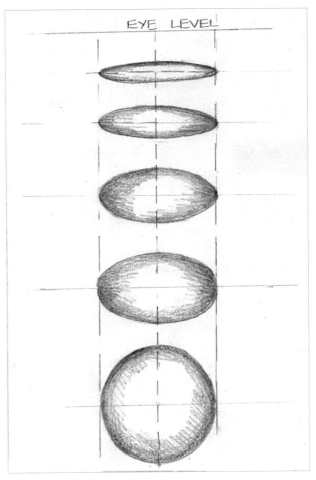

Object drawing

Learning to draw an object of any shape eventually leads to still life drawing with endless variations of shapes, colors, light and shadows. The use of various colored drawing paper, in light brown, light blue and grey, adds to the newness of the experience for the students.

A great way to begin is to have students sit in a circle and suspend a balloon from the ceiling. Darken the room as much as possible and shine a single light source on the balloon. Observing the shadow of the balloon, students can draw the rounded object as though it is hovering above the floor. This exercise can be an introduction to different media, such as charcoal pencils, Conte crayons and soft graphite pencils.

Seeing others' perspective

Students can begin to observe and understand that each drawing represents a different point of view, depending on the position of the student around the circle. This can have social ramifications and encourage a discussion of the importance of seeing another person's point of view—a critical skill for the growing teenager and for the years beyond.

Drawing "in the round"

Learning to draw round objects such as vases, cups, teapots and pitchers is a good way to introduce students to the study of perspective in seventh grade. Drawing round objects is less complex than linear perspective. With round objects, circles change to ovals in their height, not their width.

Providing the basics

In rounded objects, such as a cup, the circular shapes of the top and the base change according to the viewer's position. A basic diagram, showing eye-level and above and below views, can help students learn to draw what they see in front of them. They can practice drawing ovals and making them symmetrical. The curve of the oval at the top of the cup will be the same as the curve they see at the base of the cup. This is challenging for most students. They tend to want to draw the base as a straight line.

Measuring with the eye and the hand

Hold your arm straight out, pencil in hand and measure the height or width of the oval by visually lining up the pencil tip with the top and the thumb on the pencil barrel lining up with the bottom. This creates a measurement between the end of the pencil and the thumb. Transfer the measurement to the paper by placing the pencil down over the paper, marking off the end of the pencil with the other hand, and then marking off where the thumb is positioned, also with the other hand. (Any subsequent measurements done in this way need to be consistent with the first stretch of the arm length and the distance from the object/scene being measured.)

Begin simply

Use a simply shaped cup, preferably one without a handle. Students can progress to more elaborate shapes once they have mastered the basics.

A simple linear approach can be used as shown in the example above (right). Draw a center construction line and lightly sketch an outline of the shape of the cup. Add tones according to light and dark areas. Alternatively, draw the cup with an evenly shaded light tone, beginning in the middle and working outwards to the edges to form the cup shape. Once a simple cup has been practiced, students can more readily take up the challenge of drawing a teapot.

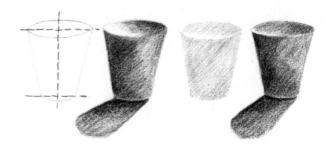

Light and shadows

Students can discuss how the light source creates a shadow on the inside of the cup on one side and a shadow on the outside of the other side of the cup, as well as a shadow on the surface where the cup is standing. This can be confusing and needs careful demonstration on the part of the teacher so that the students can understand what they see.

Cloth and folds

Learning to draw cloth is a challenging and important aspect of drawing. Begin simply with a scarf draped over a chair. Observe the shadows created by the receding folds and how the light cannot penetrate the inner recesses of the material. A scarf with a fringe adds to the variety and gives an extra challenge. Students sitting around this arrangement can again enjoy seeing the different perspectives once the drawings are hung up and viewed by everyone.

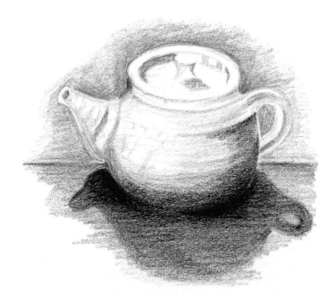

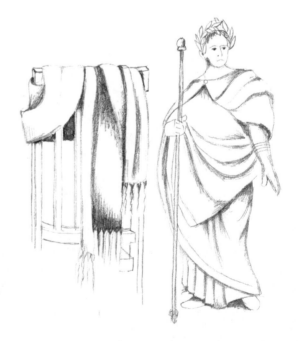

Still-life drawings

Once the students have been introduced to the basics of object drawing, they can now apply their skills to still-life compositions. Arrangements should include a variety of shapes and sizes of objects of different colors, textures and patterns. A colorful arrangement of fruit in a bowl is a great way to start. Some cloth can be added around the bowl, arranged nicely so a few folds can be seen. If the students have been introduced to drawing cloth in sixth grade, this will not be new to them and they can further hone their skills. Using colorful pastels on colored paper adds to the enjoyment and a sense of "we're doing something different." Organizing the students in groups of five or six sitting at their desks around a small table (or desk) allows them to see the arrangement from close range. This means you might need three or four bowls of fruit depending on the size of the class. It is fun to share out the fruit after they have finished their drawings, and only then!

Drawing clay solids

Drawing clay forms of solids such as cubes, rectangular or triangular solids, and cones is a great exercise to begin object drawing. The shadows thrown on the surface by the three-dimensional forms can be related to the study of light in the first block in physics.

Seventh grade

My favorite drawing experience was the pastel still-life of the fruits, bowl and cloth. It was centered on the page, accurately drawn and I was happy with the outcome.

– E.S., class of 2011

Perspective

At the age of thirteen students are really ready for the challenge of drawing in perspective. They can relate this subject to their study of the Renaissance when perspective began to appear in paintings and drawings of landscapes and buildings.

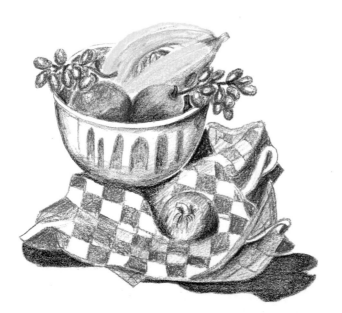

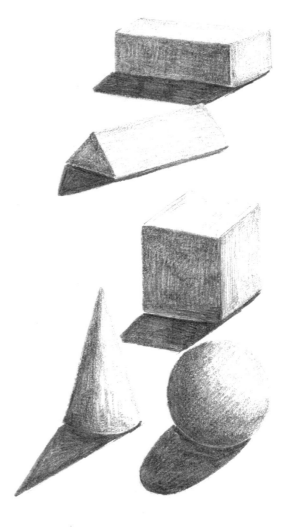

A great resource

Hermann von Baravalle's *Perspective Drawing* is a great resource for a teacher. He begins with a step-by-step guide through working with perspective divisions and trisections all the way to complex drawings of stairways, roofs, arches and cityscapes. The development and progress of the students' skills, as well as time constraints, will determine how much material can be covered in one block. Once they understand two-point perspective, the students will enjoy creating their own cityscapes, and it can be one of the culminating projects of the block. Careful and colorful shading technique can turn the buildings, spires, roof gardens and trees into magical places.

House portraits

A fun project to complement the perspective block is individual house portraits. Give the students an assignment to sketch their house, complete with notes on color, siding and trim, doors and roof and the surrounding landscaping. Suggest a simple frontal view to those who will be challenged.

Students begin their work in the classroom by lightly drawing their house from their initial sketch on watercolor or regular drawing paper. The final renderings can be done in black and white, colored pencils, pastels, watercolors or other media.

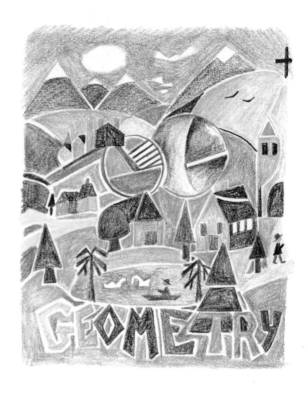

Geometry

As a contrast and as a different approach to what they experienced in sixth grade, introduce the students to working artistically with geometric shapes using pastels. They can use a ruler and a compass, but edges will not be as sharply defined as when using pointed pencils.

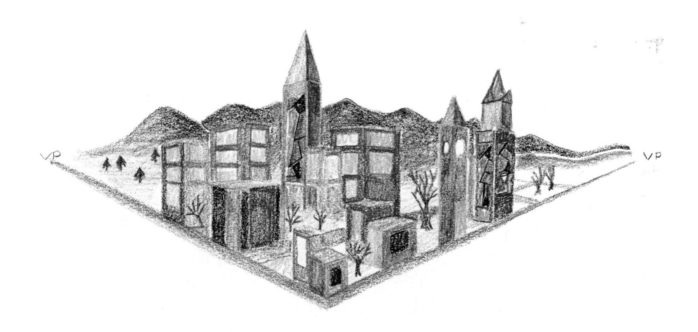

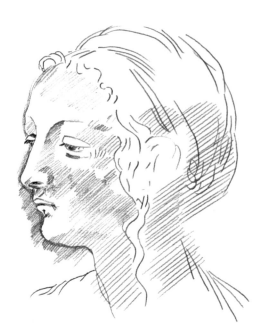

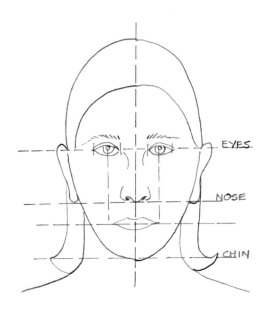

Allow the students to choose their own colors, with a limit of six in the palette to create their composition. They can use a mix of shapes that should include polygons, circles, rectangles and triangles, lines and dots. Shapes can intersect and colors can blend. Discuss the effective use of white space and the powerful effect of the use of black. In addition, address questions regarding the balance of colors in a composition.

Geometric landscapes

This can be another very popular and enjoyable assignment and offer another opportunity for very creative work. Create a landscape using only geometric shapes and natural colors, incorporating a village with a church and even people out taking a walk. Tops of trees can be triangles, as can the main body of a figure, for example.

The human face and figure

There is nothing more challenging than drawing the human face and figure. Before students are introduced to facial proportions, they will tend to draw the eyes too high up on the forehead. It takes a lot of practice to place the eyes in the midline between the top of the head and the base of the chin, to set the eyes correctly apart and to know where the ears, lips, and the base of the nose should be placed.

Once the students gain a basic understanding, they can practice by sketching each other and by drawing portraits from photographs of works of art.

Vitruvian Man

Leonardo da Vinci's famous human being inscribed in a circle and square can be studied and drawn to show the proportions of the human body.

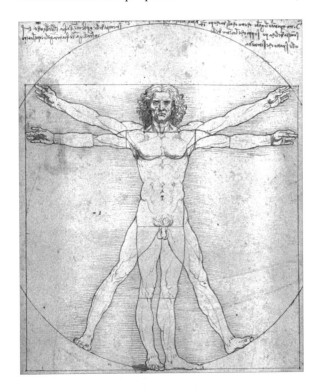

71

This is another very challenging task and, fortunately, Leonardo developed the remarkable grid with distinct measurements that can be studied and applied. Students can practice by drawing each other in simple sitting or standing positions.

The study of proportions

What I remember most is that a person is eight heads high. It wasn't something we spent time really practicing; it was mentioned a few times, but I have found it so useful!

– L.He., class of 2011

Giving students a basic knowledge of proportions in the middle school years can help them when they get to further advanced art classes in high school and beyond. In contrast to the younger years, students can now really begin to see and understand proportions in a conscious way and learn to apply new skills to their drawing.

One of the main aspects is the head size at different stages of development. Students can be shown how eight head lengths, from the top of the head to the chin, measure into the entire length of the adult human figure. Young children around age six measure the equivalent of six head lengths, while the newborn's head is huge in proportion to the length of the body, which contains only four head lengths.

It is good to periodically review proportions with the students so that the information becomes imprinted in their memory. For teachers it is helpful

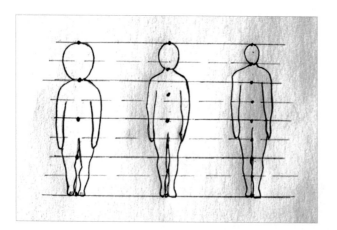

to know what makes a figure look more "childlike" or more "grownup."

Physiology

Drawing hands and feet also belongs to this year, and students don't have far to look! Drawing their left or right hand in different positions is a great way to get started. Follow this exercise by having the students place one foot on top of the desk and make a drawing. Modeling both hand and foot is equally enjoyable, doable and rewarding.

Scratchboard art

Scratchboard drawing is a challenging but most enjoyable art, and seventh grade is a perfect time to introduce the students to etching tools. By this time they are familiar with negative space and can begin to appreciate the effect of black on white paper, as well as seeing the effect of white shining out of black.

Scratchboard is a white board coated with black ink. The student will scratch away the black ink with tools, leaving the white board exposed. A variety of sizes of scratches can be made, ranging from very thin lines to those that remove large areas of black.

First some experimenting

Begin with giving out a small 5" x 6" piece of (student grade) scratchboard, whereon each student can experiment with a variety of scratches. Two students can share three basic tools: a sharp point for single, thin lines; a blunted point for thicker lines or little squares; and a roundly-cupped scraper tool that can be used for removing larger areas of black. Students will see that once the black is removed, there is no going back. Touch-ups are possible with a black fine-lined pen but are to be avoided.

A nature scene

A nature scene with trees is a good place to begin. Additional practice of trees is always beneficial, and if this project is planned for the winter months, it is a great way of drawing leafless trees. Begin with a pencil drawing, black on white, horizontal or vertical. Ask the students to incorporate a variety of

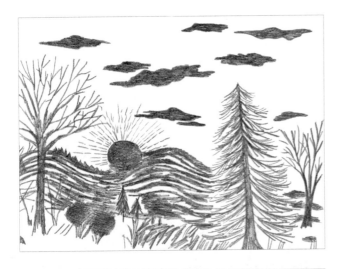

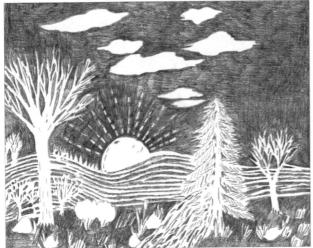

Eighth grade

Most of my favorite drawings were done in grade eight, especially portraits of famous people.

– O.K., class of 2011

Anatomy

The study of bones can be greatly complemented by drawing individual vertebrae, for example. A vertebra is full of little nooks and crannies and makes for a great study. White pencil on black paper is ideal and shows the bone in its whiteness and as negative space. Alternatively, draw the bone in negative space with black around it. An interesting assignment might be to ask the students to invent a bone shape and see what they come up with.

nature forms in their composition. Once the pencil drawings are completed, they can begin to work on the scratchboard and repeat the same landscape in reverse—white shining out of a black background.

Materials

Purchase some heavy, student-grade ink-coated paper for the experimental stage of this assignment. For the final drawing use good quality boards—it will likely make the students' work more successful. They don't have to be the best professional boards, but they should be good quality so that the lines will be cleaner and the scraped areas will not be rough. It is best to purchase some samples of boards and try them out before stocking the supplies for the class.

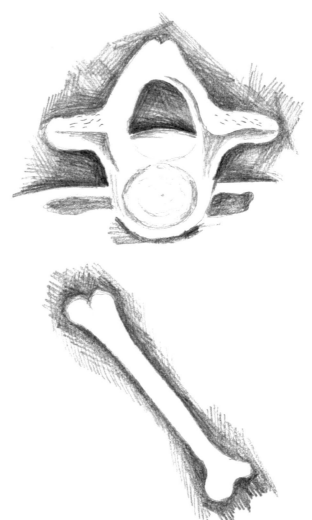

Main lesson book covers

Drawing the covers for main lesson books can be done at the end of each block. Paste them on the book covers with a margin of 1″ showing around the edges. Covers drawn with the block title and name and grade of the student can be a favorite way to end the block after all the hard work inside is done.

By eighth grade students can use their own imagination and create their own ideas for how to best represent the block. Some students will still enjoy having an example on the board to work from. Having individual covers enhances the variety of artwork done in the classroom and affords each student the opportunity to shine.

Portraits

Give students the opportunity to do a research project on an artist and to complement their study with a portrait. They can apply all the skills they have learned to try to get a recognizable likeness in their own inimitable style. In addition, give them other opportunities to create portraits. For example, they can try to get an ethnic look on a human face, such as a Vietnamese during a study on Asia, or George Washington during the American history block. Students enjoy trying to get a likeness of famous people.

Black on white diagonal-shaded drawing

The eighth grade year, especially during the winter months, is a great time to review the diagonal shading technique. This gives the students an opportunity to further develop their skills. Students were introduced to drawing with slanted lines in fourth grade, after which they moved on to shading in fifth grade. They can now attempt to keep the slanted lines separated as well as consistently angled at 45 degrees, moving from top right to bottom left with each stroke. Some students will continue to be very challenged to create even strokes, while others will pick up where they left off in earlier grades with renewed energy and capability.

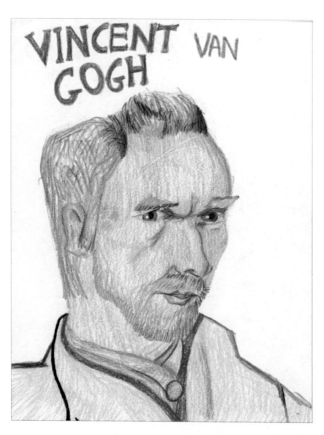

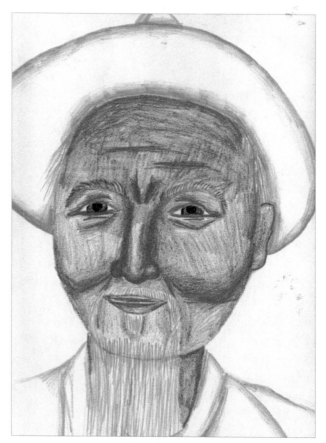

Begin simply

Begin with some simple exercises to reacquaint the students with the technique. For example, you can start with outer darkness on the periphery, moving slowly and gradually towards the center while getting progressively lighter. Leave a sphere of white in the center. Alternatively, start with a very lightly toned sphere in the middle and work towards the periphery with increasingly darker tones. For newer students who recently joined the class, this will be an entirely new and different approach to drawing. They will need a lot of guidance and support.

The fire in winter

Following this exercise, students can move on to creating a woody landscape, for example. This gives them an opportunity to practice their technique on trees, shrubs, stones, animals, figures, sticks and flames. Give students the freedom to make their drawing uniquely individual. (It cannot be emphasized enough how giving the students freedoms within limits paves the way for enthusiasm. Students can learn from each other and be inspired by others' ideas.)

Demonstrate in front of the students how to begin with the strokes at the periphery and gradually draw the darkness progressively lighter towards the fire. Once the fire is in place, other elements can be added, such as boulders and plants and figures.

Perspective lessons can be learned from hanging up the drawings and observing foreground and background as related to the position of the fire and the figures. A fire and figures positioned nearer to the front will make the elements seem closer to the viewer, whereas if the elements are set back further, they will seem more distant. Students can continue to work on positive critiquing and gaining an understanding of the importance of viewing one's work from a distance to get "perspective."

Other motifs

There are many other motifs that can be worked on. One very suitable example is to return to the cave motif that was studied in grade six in mineralogy. Instead of having a dark periphery of the sky, the

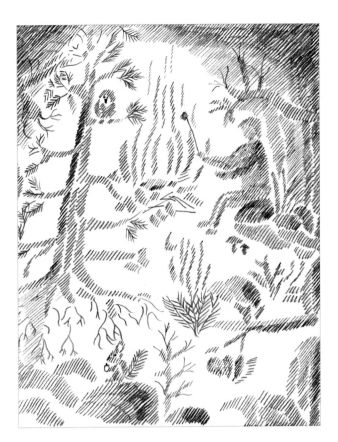

dark inside of the cave is depicted with a light source coming through an opening to the outside.

As with the fire motif, students can be free to create their own cave landscapes with stalagmites and stalactites, as well as adding human and animal forms to enliven the scene. Adding a faint horizon to be seen through the opening of the cave, with maybe some waves rolling onto a beach, completes the drawing. Hanging up the drawings and viewing them from a distance gives more opportunity for discussions on aerial perspective.

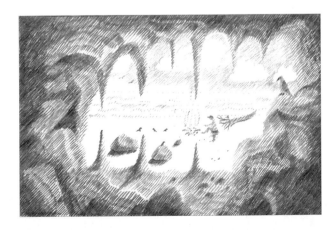

Blackboard drawing

*It has been incredibly beneficial in helping me to break away from outline drawing
and into building forms and color. It is a whole new art which I now enjoy.
And it has helped me to get into the soul of the children at different grade levels by going into their
world and drawing it the way they can see it and draw it—very powerful.
The blackboard was another great experience. I enjoyed the vivid colors and it is a medium which is
very forgiving—you can go over colors and make them disappear—it is very freeing.*

– Antioch teacher training student, 2001

The blackboard is a main feature in the Waldorf classroom. Upon entering a classroom, most often you can tell from what is on the blackboard which block is being taught. The board is a wonderful medium for writing letters and drawing images. The content on the board is easily wiped away or can remain for a period of time.

Originally blackboards were made out of slate. Nowadays blackboards are made out of a board painted in either black or green.

Different sizes and shapes

The size of the blackboard depends on the size of the classroom. In general, one of the walls of the classroom is largely taken up by one blackboard, with the rows of desks facing the board.

The blackboard can be divided with two wooden trim divisions to make it into three separate, yet joined, boards. Some blackboards are made so that the two outer divisions pivot on hinges with the middle board attached to the wall. This set-up makes it possible to open and close the outer boards and to have blackboard surfaces on both sides. Two-sided blackboards are very handy for the subject teachers who also need blackboard space to work on. Blackboards can be custom-made and shaped with angles or rounded corners to create an interesting effect in the classroom.

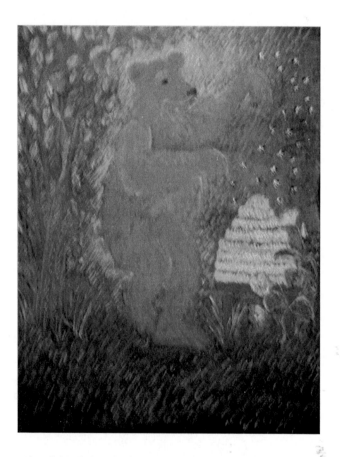

The blackboard as a writing tool

Teachers use the blackboard extensively throughout the grades. Writing can be done in any chalk color, though white shows up the best. Children also come up to the board to practice writing letters and numbers.

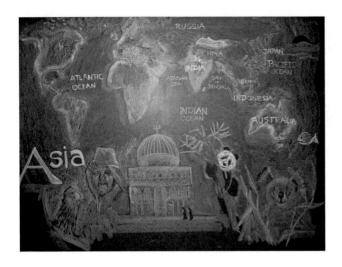

The blackboard as a drawing tool

Teachers draw extensively on blackboards in the lower grades. It is ideal for drawings to illustrate the content of the main lesson. A blackboard drawing can also give a mood of the season to the classroom and remain on the board for several weeks. In some classrooms there is a special board to the side of the room for just this purpose.

In the upper grades, a teacher may draw an image on the board that captures the essence of the block to be taught or simply write the name of the block. For example "Physics" can be written in large capital letters for a title page, with decorations all around it. It can be as elaborate as the teacher has time for, and spontaneous little illustrations can be added as the block progresses. This drawing might remain on the board for the duration of the block. It may also be replaced by other drawings pertaining to the block.

In other situations the teacher uses a certain part of the board only for drawings. Blackboard drawings can have a magic all their own and enhance the classroom experience with their beauty.

Small blackboards for form drawing

Small, individual blackboards for each student are ideal for practicing form drawing and making small sketches. They can be prepared by painting the backs of painting boards with special blackboard paint, giving the painting boards a dual purpose and saving on storage place.

Chalks for the children can be kept in small jars or boxes in their desks, and the boards can be kept at the sides of the desks or in a painting rack.

Blackboard art in the classroom

Blackboard art in the classroom has a special, unique place in the education of children in a Waldorf school. It provides an opportunity for the teacher to work in glorious color on a large format that is attached to the wall. It provides an opportunity for the teacher to bring beauty and atmosphere to the whole classroom and to join the children in celebration of the subject being studied. In addition, it provides the teacher with the opportunity to guide the children in their artwork, especially in the early grades.

Blackboard drawing in the first three grades

In the first three grades, the children are just beginning to learn to draw and can benefit greatly from guidance by the teacher. When children first learn to draw with beeswax blocks, it is better for the teacher to draw with blocks on white paper on a sketchpad resting on an easel at the front of the classroom. This will make it easier for the children to follow. The teacher uses the same size white paper as the children and the same medium. The same drawing done on a blackboard with chalks can look different, and this can be confusing for the young child.

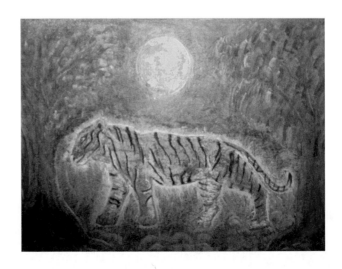

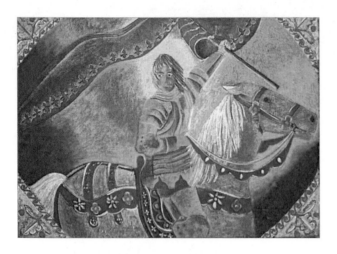

Drawing on the board in later years

As children become familiar with using the blocks and blending the colors, they become more independent and need less guidance. By third grade the teacher can comfortably draw on the blackboard and know that the students are very capable of handling the beeswax blocks and sticks. They can translate a blackboard chalk drawing into their own beeswax block drawing. They are unlikely to ask questions about what colors they should use and gradually become more immersed in their own world of color.

Approaching the large, black surface

Just as an empty white page can be intimidating, it can be daunting to the teacher to stand in front of an empty blackboard. Drawing on the blackboard is done mostly standing upright, with a tray of different colors of chalk at hand. Just as the white page is full of possibility for color, the blackboard is also full of color potential, bringing light onto a dark surface. You can think of the white paper being darkened and the blackboard being lightened, each process creating its own unique effect.

The use of chalks

It is important to use good quality chalks to ensure the achievement of bright, vivid blackboard drawings. There are several different types of chalks available for use. Mercurius chalks and Ambrite chalks are recommended.

Mercurius chalks are on the softer side and come in a range of bright colors in a box of 12. They are about 1/3" square in width and about 4" long. (They can also be used as pastel chalks for drawing on paper.) They are also available in boxes of 12 sticks of single colors.

Ambrite chalks are round and about the same width and length as Mercurius chalks. They come in boxes of 50 assorted colors or as one color only. The colors available in each brand of chalk vary. For example, among the colors in the box of Ambrite is a lovely turquoise blue, not to be found in the Mercurius selection.

Using unsuitable chalks can make for a washed-out, pale and lifeless drawing which has no shine or beauty. One important note: On no account ever use chalks that are oil-based, for they cannot be erased and will ruin the surface of the board; the board will need to be resurfaced with chalkboard paint or replaced altogether.

Where to start

Before starting a drawing on the blackboard, it is a good idea to make some small sketches first. Covering a large area of blackboard is time-consuming and, in the interest of economy of time, small sketches are the answer. They allow for a quick, simple plan of the composition, without details. They can also work as small thumbprint swatches that stir the imagination and get creative juices flowing. One sketch can lead to another and so the creative process unfurls.

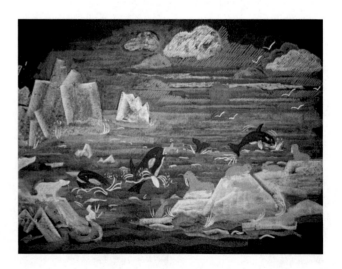

The background first

Since one layer of chalk will readily cover another layer of chalk, do the background first and then move on to the foreground. If a tree is drawn first, with the trunk and all the branches, much time will be spent afterwards in carefully filling in the sky around the branches. Much care would need to be taken not to touch the branches and cover them with blue or yellow. But when the sky is done first, the tree and its branches can be drawn straight over the blue and yellow of the sky, thus avoiding any painstaking "filling in" and any black lines and gaps where the colors come together.

Since doing the background color first is the technique for blackboard drawing, here is another reason not to draw on the blackboard in the younger grades. Working with the block crayons, the children will not do the background first, but will add it gently over and around the tree at the end. On the blackboard, blue chalk over the yellow will override the yellow and be more blue than green. But applying a yellow background with the block crayons on paper first and then wanting to create a blue form, such as a bird, will make the form green.

Applying the chalk

There are basically two different ways of applying the chalk on the blackboard. Like a beeswax stick in shape and size, the chalk can be used either flat on its side or with its tip. Applying the flat side produces a thick band of color, not unlike the effect that a beeswax block has when applied with its long side on paper. The amount of black that shows through depends on how much pressure is applied.

If the chalk is applied lightly, colors can blend well. An interesting effect can also be created when more pressure is applied to one end of the chalk than the other. This has the effect of a more intensely colored part of the tone gradually fading into a less intensely colored tone.

Diagonal shading on the board

When greater intensity of color is required, the color can be gone over once again, this time applying the diagonal shading technique. This can create a

beautiful embroidery effect, where each stroke looks like an embroidered stitch.

A lot of movement can be created by changing the direction of small, individual linear strokes. For example, the lines can move in the direction of an upward-reaching tree trunk and swirl around into the leaves and out into the sky. When the slanted lines are very similar to one another and are carefully and exactly rendered, the drawing can have a more static, orderly look.

Color combinations

It is possible to use a combination of all the colors in each drawing. Color can be used to convey different moods or to emphasize certain elements of the composition. For example, a bright golden yellow can surround a figure to give it extra focus.

Mosaic drawings

The blackboard lends itself superbly to representations of mosaics. Leaving a slight black edge around each small square that makes up the image creates the tiling effect of a mosaic quite realistically.

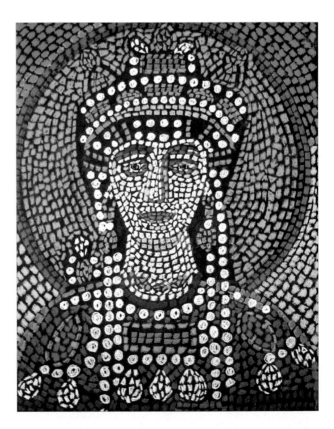

Color

*For younger children the outer and inner worlds are hardly separated.
Not only do children perceive color but also at the same time they sense its quality,
they feel in themselves its intrinsic nature, and they are conscious of the
non-material essential being of such color.*

– Brunhild Müller

Color plays an important role in the art of drawing. The study of color is complex. We see the sky in ever-changing colors—in shining blue, almost black in the night, with grey and white clouds merging into a mysterious violet, flaming up in red, glowing in yellow and orange. When we gaze around us everything comes to us in color—the white snow, the grey stone, the blue-green sea, red apples, green meadows, yellow-golden fields of corn, brown and white cows in the green meadows. Colors give infinite possibilities of expression: how they relate to one another, how different they are from one another and how each of them conveys a different mood.

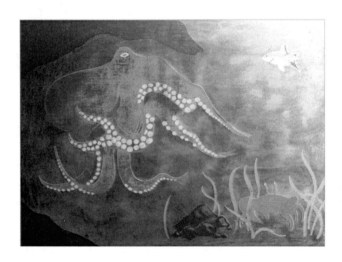

Color in the world of children

Children love colors. They love to play with colors, both in painting and drawing, and are attracted to brightly colored objects. Children are strongly affected by colors and often have one or two favorites.

Colors have attributes that make them very different and distinct from each other. Michaela Strauss (*Understanding Children's Drawings*) writes about how color can be seen as a medium of soul expression. For instance, a child has an experience and she connects a color to the nature of the experience. Yellow can be connected to a happy feeling, blue to a feeling of sadness or loneliness. The child can describe his drawing in terms of its meaning as shown by the colors.

In *Painting with Children*, Brunhild Müller describes how inner consciousness of colors is lost as children grow older and how, by the time they reach school age, they attribute colors to objects rather than soul moods.

Educating the senses

One of the ways of educating and awakening the senses is through painting and drawing with colors. In the early years it is important that children do not feel constrained into exactness by definite contours and exact forms or by the "right" colors. The forms will gradually arise out of the colors and become more important from third grade onwards.

Watercolor painting

Painting with watercolors on a wet surface gives the child an experience in the world of color that is fluid and flexible. The experience is more important than the end result. With the fluid color on the paintbrush, the child can let the color flow on the paper and make discoveries, creating stories as the painting evolves. The nature of colors can be explored fluidly, one color merging with another to create a third or fourth color.

Human soul life can be expressed through color, moods of nature as moods of the soul. Color exercises in the first three grades are the beginning of training the senses. This nourishes the child's soul and enriches the child's life. In the early grades, stories and rhymes can accompany the paintings and help the children enter into relationships with the colors.

Drawing with color

Drawing is very different from painting. The colors do not flow into each other, but can instead be applied in layers. Think of it as "painterly drawing." Instead of one color fluidly flowing into the next and creating a new third color, in drawing the colors can be created through applying one or two or several layers, one over the other.

Form through color

Painterly drawing leads the way to sculptural, three-dimensional drawing. Painterly drawing enables the young child to create form through color, colors that are translucent and have a breathing, living quality. Painterly drawing enables the child to create images in bold strokes, avoiding the exactness and focus of drawing with a line. When creating form through color, the form arises out of two different colors meeting together to form an edge.

Where two colors meet

The edge where the two colors meet can vary in its tone from being very dark to very light. Where the

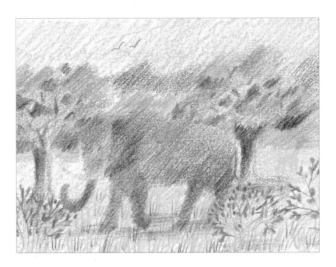

edge is dark, the two colors meet with great clarity. Where the edge is soft, the colors meet with lightness and flexibility. There is a great variety in the subtleties of how forms arise through color.

Creating flexibility

Creating form through color can, in a subtle way, enhance the drawing process and experience for both the child and the adult. If the color is initially applied gently, the forms that arise can be adjusted. In the figure to the left, a soft background of yellow is applied first. Then a soft form of an elephant arises by adding a layer of blue, beginning at the head and slowly and gradually making one's way to the tail.

At first glance one can see whether it looks good or right. The edges where the yellow meets the blue are visible yet soft and still flexible. Is the head the right size? Are the legs long enough or too long? How does the elephant look overall?

The second illustration (top right) shows additional components applied to the composition, the form of the elephant adjusted and additional shadows drawn. Because the initial tones of blue are light and the edges where the two colors meet are soft, adjustments can be made without ruining the drawing. The body can be elongated and the legs lengthened. No lines need to be erased. The elephant will not look altered.

When the initial tone is applied too heavily, adjusting the forms is more challenging. In the case of the form being too large in areas, darker tones can be

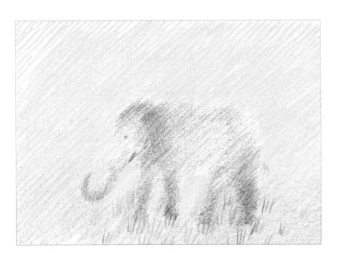

applied around them. By adding a darker tone around the shape of the elephant, the size of the animal can be reduced. For the young child this is not easy to understand. In order to take away the body mass and the length of the legs, for instance, the background color needs to become the stronger color in terms of density, so that the edge created by the blue changes. Artistic license can be invoked at times, as for instance, in creating a bush or a tree trunk just in the right spot to enhance the adjustment.

Teaching the process to children

The process of adjusting a drawing is a challenge to teach to young children. Using an eraser is a strong temptation and can be a habit from earlier years. Instead, creating form through color is an approach that is best established at the very beginning of the elementary grades. Foundations for learning are set early on and habit-forming is crucial. Children will often revert to linear drawing when left to their own devices, but this is not so in every case.

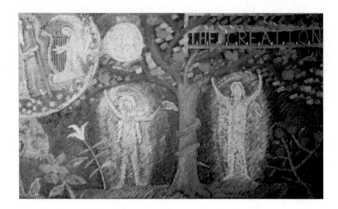

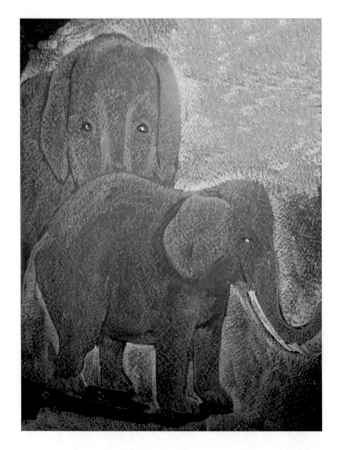

Understanding color

When awakening the children's senses through color, it is important to have a basic understanding of color and how it arises. Goethe's theory of color provides insight into the nature of colors.

Light as seen through darkness

Light seen through a partially transparent medium appears yellowish. Darkness seen through such a medium appears bluish. The archetypal instance of this phenomenon is seen in the colors of the sun and sky. Whenever we see the sun shining through a more or less clear atmosphere, the color of its disk has a tendency towards yellow, whereas the sky seen away from the sun is always bluish. When the sun is directly overhead, the darkening influence of the atmosphere is the least and the sun's light is fairly white.

Around sunrise and sunset the sun's light has to penetrate a much greater thickness of atmosphere and accordingly appears golden yellow to deep red. When the atmosphere is dry and clear, it puts little illumination between the darkness of outer space and us, and the sky appears dark, almost violet blue. At very great altitudes it can appear almost black. As the atmosphere becomes more loaded with moisture and dust particles, so the color of the sky changes from a deep blue through turquoise to pale emerald and eventually to white.

How color arises

Colors lie between light and dark. Color is either a lightening of the darkness or a darkening of the light. A landscape is most colorful in morning and evening light. The colors dissolve in the glare of noon and fade away in the blue-grey of twilight.

Yellow represents the first darkening of the light, and red is the final battle of the light to pierce through the increasing darkness. Similarly, deep violet represents the first shimmering of light which dispels the blackness, and turquoise the last vestige of color as the darkness is finally filled up with light. The warm and cold bands of colors represent the birth of color out of light and darkness. *Green* is where the two opposite bands balance one another.

Colors in relation to light and darkness

WHITE is the experience that comes nearest to the nature of light that in itself is invisible.

YELLOW stands next to whiteness. It has the greatest radiating power and the greatest susceptibility to impurity. It has hardening and formative influences and represents the first stage of the darkening of light.

ORANGE represents the middle stage of the darkening of light. It is a strong color, with increasing energy.

RED (scarlet) is light nearly overcome by darkness. Red expresses this battle in its greatest violence. There is maximum energy and maximum obstruction. As a light it represents violence, wrath and warning. The darkening influence within the light is very strong—it is the most aggressive color and produces the strongest after-image.

VIOLET-BLUE stands next to darkness. Most mysterious of all the colors, it has the least radiating power. It is hard to produce in real purity.

TURQUOISE-BLUE is the most negative and retiring color and produces the least after-image.

GREEN is pre-eminently a balance between the activity of yellow and the passivity of turquoise. The darkening of these two colors produces it. The darkening of the yellow hardens the formlessness of the turquoise. The result has the effect of inertness. The Earth's green, tranquil cover expresses this.

MAGENTA is a balance between red and blue; the blue softens and lightens the fierceness of red. Goethe called this color *peach blossom*. It is a balance to the green of nature. Magenta, if used as an extended material surface, can be unbearable.

CRIMSON is the color of deep rose, scarlet tamed by the gentle softening influence of blue.

BLACK is the absence of light. Its representative is most commonly carbon in the form of coal or charcoal. Interestingly, the crystal-clear diamond is a hard form of carbon, and the carbon arc lamp gives the whitest light that man can produce.

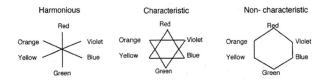

The color circle

Goethe arranged the colors in a six-fold circle and developed his theory of harmony. When the human eye is surrounded by color, it becomes active and instinctively produces the opposite color—the complementary color. Red produces green, yellow produces violet; blue, orange, and vice versa. The colored after-image together with the given color always produces the totality of the whole color circle.

Harmonious, characteristic and non-characteristic colors

Goethe's research led him to the theory of the law of all harmony, where the corresponding color pairs in the circle are called harmonious.

The second principal classification is characteristic colors. As you travel around the color circle, you arrive at these when you leave out one color and arrive at the next—red-yellow, yellow-blue, blue-red. The characteristic color combinations of the circle all give different impressions. Yellow and blue contain the contrast between radiance and shade, yellow and red express gaiety and splendor. All these

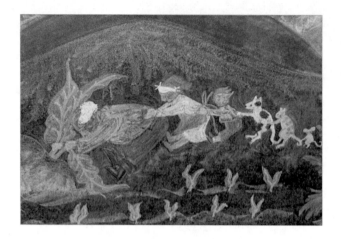

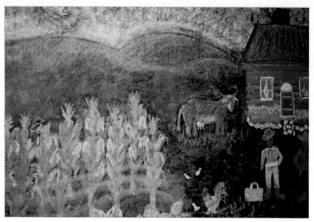

color combinations lack the third color. They mix together to arrive at a balance, which produces three additional pairs of colors: orange-green, green-violet, violet-orange.

A final grouping results from taking the color pairs that are next to each other in the circle: yellow-orange, green-blue, violet-red, and so forth. This group is called the non-characteristic color combination for they are too close to each other to produce a noticeable effect.

The qualities of colors

Colors can be described to have qualities or moods. Yellow can appear cheerful, happy and radiant but also magnificent. Blue is shy, receding, repellent, reserved. Green can be seen as peaceful, calm, joyful and fresh; orange as friendly, brave and vigorous; red as royal, majestic, festive, and so on.

The experience of color is important for the growing child—to immerse herself in the element of feeling brought on by the colors. Goethe draws our attention to the feelings that arise in us through colors. He points to the challenging nature of red and the stillness and contemplation of blue. As teachers we can present the colors to children in such a way that they will spontaneously experience the shades of feeling engendered by the colors. They will naturally feel the quality of the colors.

The color story

In the early grades the teacher can bring about, in an imaginative way, awareness in children of the different relationships to color. This can be done through telling and painting color stories.

The colors come alive and speak to each other in a reverent, innocent manner. The exercises are done slowly so that a deep impression is made on the children. This experience of color and the harmonious combinations awakens in children a sense of aesthetics and beauty.

The qualities of color in drawing

In drawing, especially in the earlier grades, the qualities of colors can also, to a significant extent, enhance the content and meaning of the story. For example, a peacefully settled cow in the field can be given a bluish, restful color, and a horse that runs all over the field can be given a reddish brown, active color. The artist Franz Marc provides an interesting example in one of his paintings of horses. The painting is extraordinary in that it has one blue and two red horses. A blue horse! Yet the blue horse next to its red companions gives an impression of gentle peacefulness.

In a similar manner, a grey stone can become bluish purple, and a distant mountain range can have some purple tones added. A tree trunk can come alive with hues of yellow, orange, green and blue with a tinge of red. Playing with colors can enhance the experience of the world of the young child and stimulate the imagination.

The use of black in drawing

In painting through the beginning grades in a Waldorf school, the three primary colors are used and secondary colors are created. Bringing all the colors together creates a rich, dark brown. Black, in its truest blackness, is absent from these paintings. In drawing, through the beginning grades, the colors representing the whole spectrum are used: red, orange, gold, yellow, green, blue and purple. Bringing all the colors together by placing one layer over another eventually brings about a very dark, blue-brown color that is close to black. When all the colors come together, they resolve into the darkness.

Black in nature and its use in the classroom

Very little, if anything, in nature is truly black. Even a crow or raven has tinges of blue in its feathers. Black can be appropriately used in drawing in the classroom for special touches: for example, a crow or ants in an Aesop's fable in the second grade, hair for a Native American tale in third grade and the ravens whispering in Odin's ears in fourth grade. Black also has its definite place, purpose and importance in the middle school and high school years.

Interestingly, when black is made available in addition to colors, it tends to dominate the drawing, especially if it is generously or excessively used. The eye tends to focus and linger on it and the rest of the images in the picture recede.

Making black available

Children are often mysteriously drawn to black and according to Audrey McAllen, a remedial specialist from Great Britain, "black signifies bone structure. Through this color children perceive their physical body." She writes that black is an important color and children should have access to it so that with it they can express their first awareness of their physical body.

A healthy child uses black exactly at the right place, time and in proportion. A child too embedded in the mechanical movements of the body uses black disproportionately, constantly and in excess.

Making possible the use of black without restraints is necessary when children draw during an assessment in the early school years, and perhaps at other stages in the early grades, but generally in classroom drawing it is advisable to limit it to appropriate use.

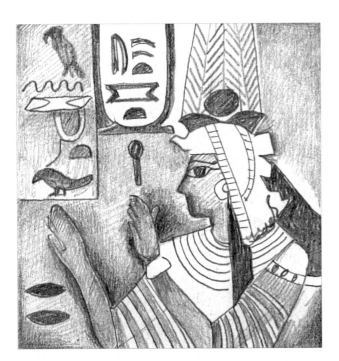

Practical advice

I happen to draw with a pen, my favorite tool. Maybe you'll like a pencil better, or chalk, or a brush. You will only find out what is best for you by trying all of these. You'll discover a paper that is exactly right for you as you try all kinds of paper, from Manila to cheap newsprint to the finest Japanese.

– Frederick Franck

There are many practical aspects to consider when drawing, as well as a great variety of materials.

The use of paper

Paper is the most frequently used medium for drawing in the classroom. There are many different types, weights and colors to choose from. The weight of the paper, its thickness and its texture are important criteria. The weight of paper is measured in pounds (lbs) or grams (gms). The thicker and heavier the paper, the more texture it has. A 50 or 55 lb. paper is recommended for drawing. This weight of paper provides a smooth surface for drawing. Experimenting with papers of different weights will show the results. In some respects a lot of texture has its own distinct beauty.

Different colored paper

White paper is the most commonly used in the classroom. A white background can give drawings a sparkle as it shines through the colors.

Black paper is wonderful to use in its own way. The teacher can use it to make sketches in preparation for a blackboard drawing or use it in the middle school years for students to work on with white or color pastels.

Brown paper can also be very effectively used in the middle and high school, with either black or white Conte crayons or pastels.

Colored construction paper is mostly used for collage and other art projects, but can add variety to drawing either with graphite pencils, colored pencils, ink or pastels.

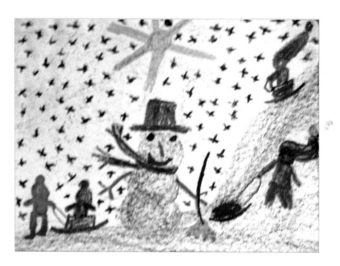

Main lesson books

In Waldorf schools, the main lesson books created by the children are one of the most important artistic elements of the education. In them the children record the lesson content, with drawings accompanying the writing. The books contain the students' own essays, poems and reflections on, for example, science experiments.

In the lower grades the books are usually a large size of 14" x 17" (horizontal format), and gradually the size is reduced so that by the time the students are in eighth grade, the page size is 8½" x 11" (vertical format). These books are a student-made record of all the subjects taught throughout the eight years of elementary education (see "Drawing in main lesson books").

In the beginning years the drawings are large and accompany the large first letters. In subsequent years, the format of the book shrinks in size, pictorial

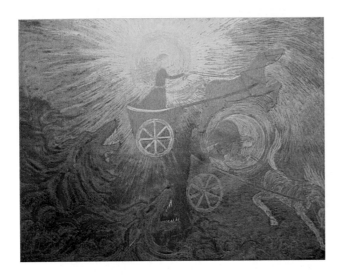

content diminishes in size, the writing becomes progressively smaller and the amount of writing increases.

Drawing media

There are many different drawing media to use with a variety of drawing approaches. The most widely used medium in the early grades in Waldorf schools is the beeswax block and stick crayons. These crayons come in an array of bright colors. Originally they were designed for use by older children, but they lend themselves well to painterly drawing in broad strokes for the young child.

In first grade the students are often provided with only eight colors—lemon yellow, gold, orange, vermilion (orange-red), carmine (red), blue, dark green and purple. However, a fuller spectrum of colors can also be provided. Students will have the use of light green, several shades of brown, black, white, grey and pink.

The use of beeswax crayons

Beeswax crayons are a unique medium. The shining brightness of the colors, combined with the look that can be achieved by applying the wax block to the surface of the paper, gives a translucent breathing quality to the drawing. This is especially so when the wax is applied in gradual layers, becoming richer in tone with every layer applied.

In the process of applying the layers, there comes a point when the paper surface becomes saturated with wax and the tiny pores of light shining through from the paper become obliterated. At this point the surface area covered has become opaque and the translucency is lost. Other colors in layers underneath can no longer be seen. There is a delicate balance of how many layers to apply and when to stop before the saturation point has been reached.

Layering with different colors

Beeswax crayons lend themselves well to mixing colors together to create more color combinations. For example, the trunk of a tree can be brought imaginatively alive by applying several layers of colors to produce a rich brown. You can begin with orange as a base color, followed by vermilion, blue, green and even purple. In this way a tree trunk can be made up of five different layers of beeswax, all shining through each other, one layer placed on top of another. With this method the brown has been created. It has a very different look and feel than that provided by the brown directly from a brown crayon.

Experimenting with color combinations

Combining different colors produces a varied palette. Experimenting with combining different colors can be done separately on a practice sheet before beginning to draw.

Begin by making a swatch of every color in the beeswax crayon palette. Then step by step, combine each color with all the other colors. For example, try lemon yellow with gold, with orange, with vermilion, with carmine, with blue, with green, with purple. Make combinations with three colors, checking to see what the difference is when one color or the other is applied first or last. Each color shines through to the next, some colors being or becoming more dominant.

Children drawing with blocks

There are several ways of applying layers of colors with the rectangular blocks. Strokes can be applied mostly with the short end of the rectangle. The stroke itself can be made in several directions including up and down, horizontally back and forth and diagonally back and forth. The colors can be made darker by

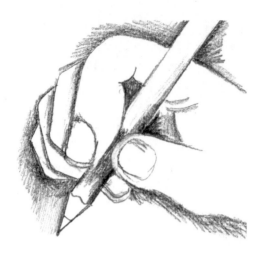

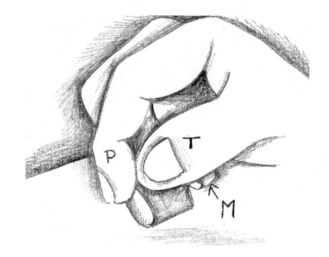

applying pressure and covering the area with many layers of wax until the paper is saturated and almost opaque.

The importance of the right grip

The teacher needs to ensure that young children use the correct finger grip when using beeswax block and stick crayons and, later, pencils. The correct finger grip should be encouraged from the very beginning and the teacher can show and demonstrate this in front of the children by holding up a pencil. The pointer finger and thumb essentially *hold* the pencil while the middle finger *supports* the pencil.

It is equally important for children to hold the block in the right way. This needs vigilance by the teacher as children can slide into uncomfortable, unsuitable grips that make it awkward for them to use the blocks and sticks as well as affect their pencil grip. The illustrations show grips that are comfortable for the hand and most similar to a pencil grip while holding the blocks.

The motion of the strokes can go back and forth, up and down, horizontally back and forth left and right. The block should be held with the pointer, the thumb, and middle finger, much like holding a pencil or a paintbrush. The illustration below shows an awkward grip with the block held in a cramped manner.

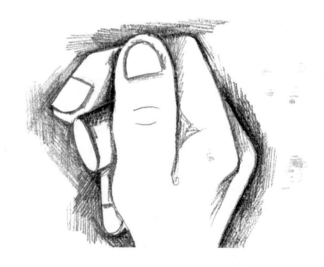

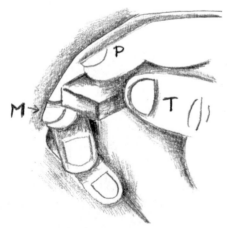

P = pointer, T= thumb, M = middle finger

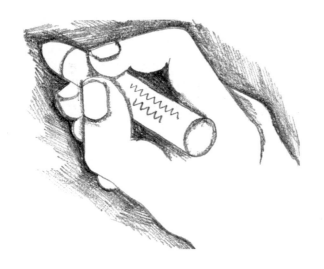
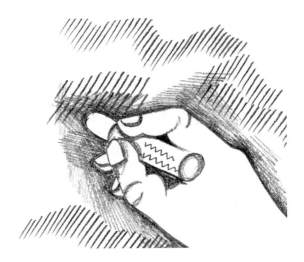

Using the block as a writing tool

The beeswax block was not designed as a writing tool and should be used only for drawing. Using beeswax blocks for writing may cause unhealthy development of the muscles, nerves and tendons.

The blocks are sometimes used to draw very large capital letters or forms in the first grade when the children are first learning to write the alphabet. This should be an exception and kept to a minimum.

Writing with beeswax sticks

Beeswax sticks can be used for writing large letters in the first two grades. The grip on the beeswax stick crayon is much the same as the grip on a pencil. The sticks also lend themselves well to drawing linear forms. In addition, sticks can be used for adding detail to a block drawing or solely on their own for drawing with the slant line technique.

When used for writing in particular, it is better not to use the sticks if they are too worn down or short and stubby. The stick needs to rest comfortably on the pointer finger just ahead of the knuckle. For writing more than a few sentences, it is preferable for the child to use a thick, long, pencil. The pencil rests more fully on the space between the thumb and the pointer finger.

Drawing with a slanted line

In addition to drawing details, the sticks can also be used for creating the surrounding environment, such as the earth and the sky. When drawing with blocks, the area is painted in broad strokes. When drawing with sticks in slanted lines, the strokes are applied with a blunt point, which results in fairly thin lines. Creating tones on the page with the sticks takes longer and requires many more movements of the arm. The quality of the tone created by the sticks on the paper depends on how the sticks are applied (see "Diagonal-shaded drawing").

Colored pencils

Colored pencils are a staple of the Waldorf school classroom, sometimes even as early as third grade. Drawing with pencils makes it possible for the young artist to create both large areas of tone as well as exact detail.

There are many different types of colored pencils and it is best to sample some to check out their quality. Look for colored pencils that are very soft and gentle and easy to work with, for both children and adults. The box sizes range from 12 to 100 pencils. A box of twenty-four colors is sufficient. The soft pencils can also be purchased in the form of sticks, about a quarter inch square by three inches long. These are very handy; they have no wood around them and so do not need much sharpening.

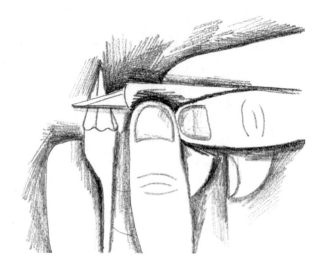

Sharpening pencils

Soft colored pencils tend to break easily within the wooden shaft that covers them. Care needs to be taken that they do not fall on the floor. They can be problematic to sharpen and often break more easily using a regular pencil sharpener. Sharpening with a small knife kept at the teacher's desk is a preferred way of sharpening.

Since children cannot keep Exacto or other knives at their desks, the teacher will need to perform this function for them. The pencils tend to break less and this method is generally not as frustrating except that it makes more mess with little wooden pencil shavings flying off the pencil. Another alternative is to sharpen the pencil on a piece of sandpaper.

Graphite pencils

Formerly referred to as lead pencils, the graphite pencil is the everyday pencil in common use everywhere. It often comes with an eraser at one end and, if used lightly, any mark made can be erased almost entirely. The lighter the mark, the more chance there is to make any adjustment. This medium is very versatile and can be used for many purposes. Graphite pencils come in varying degrees of softness and hardness. Hard pencils are ideal for writing, whereas the soft ones are better for drawing. A very soft pencil can almost give the effect of a charcoal drawing. When purchasing, H stands for "hard" and B stands for "soft," with the degree of hardness and softness referred to by numbers.

Pastels

Pastels generally come in two kinds, chalk and oil pastels. Chalk pastels are the more versatile of the two. They can be applied lightly and blended into each other. You can use the tips of your fingers to blend and smooth chalk pastels. The resulting surface tone is soft, and if not too much pressure is applied, some of the white paper can still shine through.

Oil pastels come in bright, vivid colors that are much the same as chalk pastels, but they are in some respects less versatile. It is a challenge to blend one color into another, and there is less possibility for translucency. Oil pastels bring a unique quality to a drawing.

Conte crayons

Conte crayons are similar to oil pastels except that they are available in shades of black, brown and white. Conte crayons, once applied, are permanent on the paper, and it is a challenge to adjust what has been applied. Conte crayons are a messy medium and great care needs to be taken not to smudge the work while drawing.

When using Conte crayons on paper, it is recommended that the artist sit with the sketch pad at an angle as shown, so that the arm is free of the paper and less likely to smudge what is underneath. It is recommended to start lightly with the lightest tones and build from there, so that there is possibility for adjusting the forms. Once applied too darkly there is little room for adjustment.

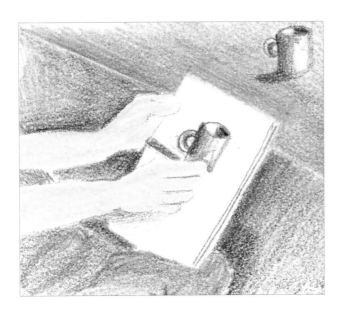

Drawing at a surface angle

Placing the sketchpad at an angle is also a comfortable way to draw, regardless of the medium used. The teacher can introduce this in middle school art classes when doing object drawing, for example. It is recommended that the angle of the surface be similar to the angle of the head as it looks down on the paper. However, it would not be suitable for children working in their main lesson books every day. It certainly helps to have school desks with adjustable tops.

Charcoal

Charcoal is similar to chalk pastels when it is applied. Charcoal is black and is usually available in long, thin sticks or in pencil form. Charcoal applies easily with little pressure and can be smoothed and moved around with a finger. It is an extremely messy medium and great care needs to be taken to not smudge the paper while working and after the work is completed. To protect the finished work a fixative spray can be applied.

Charcoal is ideally suitable for black and white studies, for example, human figure drawing. Its depth of tone can range from the lightest grey to the darkest black.

Magic markers

Magic markers usually come in very bright and intense colors in sets of twelve or more. The medium is like fluid ink inside a casing with a felt-type dispenser at the tip.

Markers are very versatile and easy to use for making charts and using on specialized boards from which the marker can be wiped off clean without a trace. When used on porous paper, they tend to be permanent, penetrating deeply, and cannot be erased. They can be wonderful for making designs and linear patterns.

Magic markers do not lend themselves to tentative exploration of shapes and forms. Once the marker has made its mark, it is there to stay. There is no possibility for adjustment. The colors tend to be opaque and lack translucency. It is challenging to blend one color with another. The edges of colors, when placed next to each other, tend to be hard.

Additional drawing tips

Art is about openness, about letting go of the old and discovering the new.
It is also about play. Art encourages children into play through the magic of colors,
through the nature of different substances in modeling,
and into the drama of light and darkness, form drawing and elements of the crafts.

– Margrit Jünemann and Fritz Weitmann

There are many ways teachers can be empowered to draw with students in a classroom setting. The various aspects of drawing can be challenging, especially for the new teacher. Many adult students, training to become teachers, have not done any drawing since the middle school grades. Many have never had any formal or informal drawing practice. For years many of them have been afraid of and anxious about drawing and have done little or no artistic activity.

For adults, linear representation is often the preferred approach to drawing. For many adults their single experience has been the outline approach. Drawing with a slanted line or with a breathing tone can come as a true revelation. It can result in a complete turnaround and bring a new lease on their creativity. They realize, after all and to their great surprise, that they are able to create artwork of beauty. This revelation can be life-changing.

Picture building

Many teachers new to storytelling experience challenges with their "inner picture" building. They do not readily see the images in the story in their mind's eye, in their imagination.

The use of small sketches

One way to stimulate the imagination is to read a short story and make small, thumb-size, five-minute sketches. Do the sketches in simple images with broad surface tones and shapes without detail, so that the emphasis is on placing the various elements of the composition in a balanced way. Try a succession of

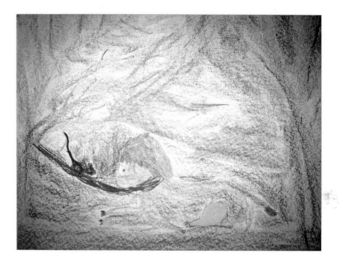

four or five sketches depicting significant scenes or events. The composition that depicts the essence of the story could then be the one chosen to do with the students.

Economy of time

There is much to do in the life of a teacher and economy of time is essential in order to meet the demands of the work. Particularly for this reason it is advisable to keep the sketches really simple and avoid spending any time on encumbering details.

Practicing broad areas of tone and simple shapes can become a very helpful way of "seeing things" in a short amount of time. At the preparation stage of small sketches, details can be kept to a minimum. Redo the small sketch on larger, classroom-size paper later. With practice you will become adept at creating images and being able to draw in front of the children.

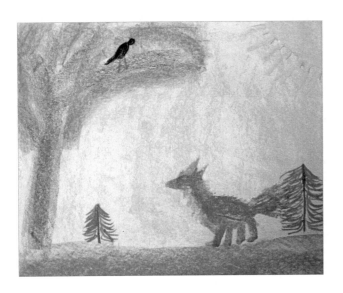

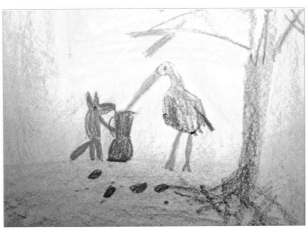

Drawing in front of the children

Drawing in front of the children is an important aspect of the classroom work in the lower grades. In the beginning of a new teacher's work in the classroom, this can be a daunting prospect that needs good preparation. Basically there are three approaches. You can make sketches at home, choose one, draw it on classroom-size paper, bring it in to the classroom and hang it up when it is time to draw. Or you can leave the large-size drawing at home and draw from memory with the students in the classroom. Once you become adept at drawing, the images may even appear "off the cuff."

Drawing step by step

In the very beginning, when drawing in front of the children, talk about the steps you are taking while drawing. For example, *"First we will begin by taking our dark green block crayon and making the grass grow down here below on the earth. Then we will bring some lemon yellow over the grass. As you can see, the sun is shining."* This is an organic, natural approach. Start from the ground upward, establishing the space into which the content will be placed. Grow the trees and plants from the roots upwards, following the natural process of growth.

Draw animals and human beings from the head downwards, according the head the dignity of being considered first. Follow up with a body that supports it.

Drawing animals and human beings

Much has already been said about drawing animals. The more time you spend practicing animal shapes the better.

From my observation in second grade, anxiety over animal shapes and how to draw them begins at this stage of children's development. A great deal depends on you and how you help the children overcome their anxiety. Allowing children to practice on extra sheets of paper before they do the final picture in their books is a good idea, especially for those children for whom the anxiety over drawing animal shapes is strong and can be overwhelming.

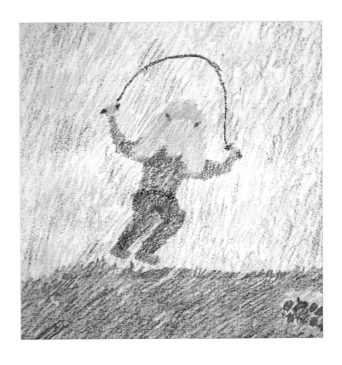

The human figure

When drawing human figures with young children, it is important to consider lightly drawing the whole shape first, before "putting on the clothes." This gives the students the foundation of the human figure upon which clothes are placed, rather than a head sticking out of a shirt and feet protruding from a pair of pants. It also helps the young child see where and how the different parts of the body are connected and what the form is under the clothes. Drawing the clothes first can create a rather discombobulated figure. Feet can protrude in a way that does not correspond to the rest of the body.

For example, when drawing a queen lying under a quilt on a bed, draw the bed first. Draw her whole body lying on the bed, and then draw a quilt covering her. This way the students can experience the whole body lying under the quilt. This is preferable to drawing her head on the pillow, the quilt covering up the rest of the body and her feet sticking out at the end.

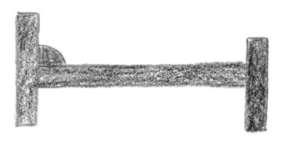

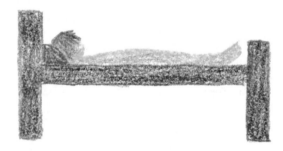

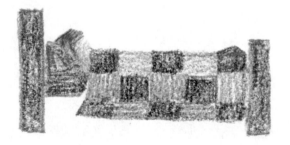

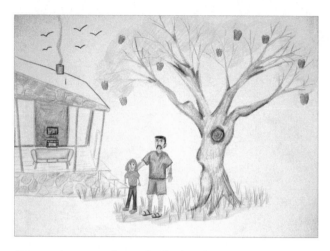

Shaping out the whole body

Once the drawings of the children become more sophisticated, it becomes more important to focus on the proportions of the body. As with animals, the human form is challenging to draw and can become a lifelong study. Begin by drawing the head, moving down the neck, over the shoulders and down the arms, finishing up with the trunk and finally the legs and feet.

Drawing so that the children can see

Standing in front of the class and enabling the children to see what you draw needs careful consideration. When drawing with the right hand, it is comfortable to stand on the left side of the page. A left-handed teacher stands on the right side. You can also draw from below in a sitting position, but this can be a strain on neck and arms.

Not being able to stand straight in front of what you are drawing is a challenge and takes practice, since it is difficult to see exactly what you are doing from an angle. At times it will be necessary to stand back from the drawing to check on its progress.

Independent drawing

Once the children have established a firm grasp of spatial orientation on the page, are familiar with the drawing medium and have a good sense for composition, the teacher's role in drawing in front of the class can begin to lessen. For many students it remains necessary for the teacher to be an ongoing guide, yet independence and creativity should be encouraged at all times. Students will, of themselves, creatively add components out of their own imagination.

At times, students will feel the need to add components that are not appropriate to the subject matter at hand. You can gently but surely steer them away from going in this direction.

Free drawing

The question often comes up whether to allow students in a classroom setting to draw whatever they like during free drawing time. Some teachers give each student a special book for free drawing. You may need to establish some guidelines as to what is appropriate in the educational setting.

Taking the time

It takes time to do a drawing of quality. Students gradually develop a sense of aesthetics. Especially in the beginning grades, while laying the foundation and while the students' imitation capability is still so strong, the way the teacher draws by example is of paramount importance.

Throughout the grades the teacher can serve as an example and show how tones can be drawn with beauty and care. Taking care over a sky or background is equally as important as drawing the main elements of the composition. A carelessly scribbled background can spoil a lovely drawing, no matter how carefully the main elements of the picture are rendered.

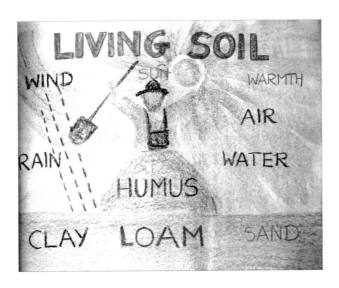

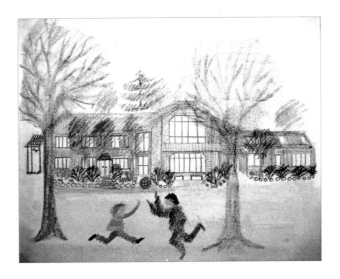

Translating the work of others

Ideas for drawing in the classroom can also be inspired from already existing works of art or illustrations in books pertaining to the subject matter. This is especially so in the later grades when the students are studying history. Black and white illustrations can be translated into colorful compositions. Elements can be taken from certain artworks and recomposed specifically for the subject at hand. Rather than copying the ready-made artwork verbatim, translating elements from it makes it into a personalized drawing.

Learning from works of art

The teacher can learn much from studying works of art. Drawing from a painting or etching can be a stimulating experience, and much appreciation can be gained for different styles and techniques. Studying the history of art in its rich diversity and broad ranges of aesthetics is highly rewarding. Viewing and meditating on a painting, drawing or sculpture can be an extremely inspiring experience, and can help educate the eye to observe proportions, light and shadows.

Allowing enough time

It is essential that teachers, in particular new teachers, give themselves time to become practiced and confident in their artwork. Just as learning to master an instrument takes ongoing practice, it may

95

take years of drawing before the teacher becomes comfortable with it. Being comfortable in front of the children goes a long way towards the success of any drawing lesson.

Much can also be learned from appreciating the styles and ways of drawing of colleagues at a school or other students in the training. Seeing other students' work is an important part of the preparation for classroom drawing. Learning to see what works well and what can be improved upon is part of this process.

Learning to give positive criticism and feedback goes along with the creative process. It is also important to be able to be objective about one's own work, to appreciate it and to see what areas need improvement.

Education as an art

The premise that education is an art calls on all teachers to be artists—a challenging call! Each teacher must strive to realize this goal in her individual way. Artistry needs to be awakened and nurtured in a delicate manner so that it can flourish and grow in its capacities and, in so doing, enrich people's lives. Through the arts, healing can be found.

Working with a breathing tone can foster and bring about this possibility of healing. Focus on simple and generalized shapes and avoid falling into the trap of detail. Drawing can be a satisfying and re-enlivening experience.

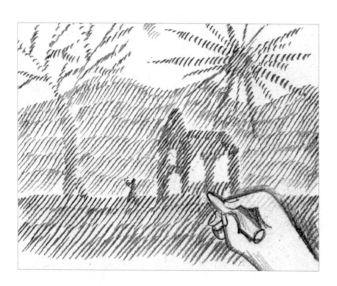

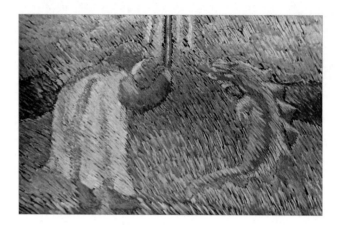

Left-handedness

Although the majority of teachers are right-handed, there are usually one or two left-handed teachers in each group of teachers, just like there are left-handed students in each classroom. Left-handed teachers often have questions regarding their own left-handedness and that of the children they will teach.

If we consider the social history of using the left hand or the right, we find that Chinese paintings and also cave paintings were largely created with the left hand. Writing was also initially done with the left hand, only gradually changing to the right; and there is the famous stone from the 5th century BC where the Greek letters meander, going from left to right and right to left, changing all the time. We thus see an evolution from left to right when writing became of prime importance in civilization, and right-handedness came increasingly to the fore.

– Michaela Glöckler, MD
Aspects of Left-handedness

The question of dominance

The questions of dominance and laterality are of singular importance for the child and will need to be studied by the teacher. Much has been written about this subject, including the teaching of a left-handed child to write with the right hand. (Articles for further reading and study are included in the bibliography.)

Any questions a teacher or home-schooling parent may have regarding a child's mixed dominance or left-handedness should be discussed in a broader way with colleagues or other consultants. Mixed dominance can sometimes lead to learning challenges. Strengthening one-sided dominance or even changing dominance from left to right needs very careful consideration. In most schools children who write and draw with their left hand are free to use their preferred hand, and changing dominance from left to right is no longer practiced as it was in former times.

The study of left-handedness

Left-handedness is a fascinating study and it behooves all teachers to try to understand the significance of right, left or mixed dominance and how dominance is established in the early years. The small percentage of left-handed students in each class deserves particular understanding and appreciation.

Over the ages there has been a cultural significance of left-handedness that still lingers in today's world, where right-handedness is the norm and connotations of good and bad, right and wrong continue to reverberate.

Special considerations

Left-handed students will need special consideration, at the very least some recognition that their left-handedness is not in any way a disability or a sign of dysfunction. Left-handed students and right-handed students are on equal terms in the classroom. Genuinely left-handed students often display evidence of artistic ability and musicality.

One of the most artistic students in my class was a left-handed girl who illustrated her main lesson books profusely and with great style. In addition she could "see" perspective already in third grade, and she lived strongly in her imagination right up through middle school.

The left-handed teacher

The left-handed teacher has a distinct disadvantage as well as a great advantage in the classroom. The disadvantage presents itself mostly in the first two years when first and second grade students are learning to read and write, and the majority of the students will be right-handed. Once the foundation of writing and reading is firmly established, the students will no longer depend as much on the example set before them by the teacher, who can then be freer to write or draw with her left hand.

The advantage is that a left-handed teacher can fully demonstrate writing and drawing for the left-handed student in the first two years when they need the most guidance and assistance. This undoubtedly affords an advantage to the minority of the students in the class and helps to make the connection special.

Drawing in front of the children

The left-handed teachers surveyed for the purposes of this book all demonstrated writing with their right hands during first grade. They recommend this to other left-handed teachers despite the fact that some of them experienced moderate difficulties. One teacher managed to write equally well with both hands. This practice did not appear to affect her left-handed writing.

Drawing with the right hand for a left-handed teacher is also a considerable, if not greater, challenge. David Mitchell, former class teacher and high school teacher, said, "As a class teacher I took great pains, in my two first grade classes, to write with my right hand only while at the blackboard, as well as drawing forms. However, I could draw pictures only with my left! Usually I always placed my drawing on the board the night before so I could work with it until I was reasonably satisfied." Another teacher shared that she, too, always tried to draw on the board with her right hand in first and second grades but was not always able to do so.

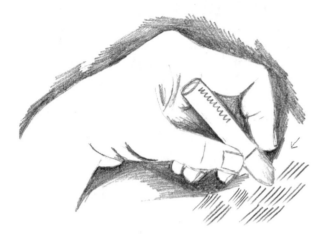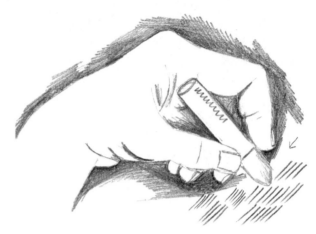

Diagonal shading

While for right-handed students the strokes will be drawn from top right to bottom left, the left-handed students will have a choice of direction, depending on how they write and draw. They will either bend the wrist and extend the elbow upwards and create the slant line from top right to bottom left, or they will hold the hand in a more relaxed, straight-forward manner and create the lines from top left to bottom right. The bent wrist/extended elbow position sometimes evolves from the student's not wanting to smear ink while moving the hand.

Teacher demonstration

While introducing diagonal-shaded drawing in fourth grade, it is advisable to demonstrate both of the following ways for left-handed students—strokes from the top right to bottom left and strokes from the top left to the bottom right. The right-handed students will draw the strokes from top right to bottom left.

Classroom research

Art with all its variety and manifestations can become a fascinating and helpful study in any classroom. To delve into the various areas of development in art gives new meaning and understanding to child growth, which is dynamic.

– Viktor Lowenfeld

A fundamental task of teachers is to endeavor to understand the children they teach in the classroom. There are many aspects of the developing child to consider, including family history, physical description, movement, academic and artistic strengths, and so forth. The activity of drawing is also an important one.

My classroom research is based on Audrey McAllen's indications for the "Person, House, Tree" drawings and their analysis, as well as what I have observed in the classroom throughout the elementary school years. At the beginning, in the middle, and at the end of each of the eight years, all the children in my class were asked to draw a "Person, House, Tree" picture.

Observations

In between the assignments of the "Person, House, Tree" drawings, I watched the children draw in their main lesson books. Observing the development of a personal style was a particularly interesting part of the study, as well as observing developments in capability as the years went by.

The influence of the teacher on children was another aspect of the research, as well as observing drawings of children who came from other schools in the middle of first grade and in subsequent years.

The history of analysis

Children's drawings have been the subject of many specialists dating all the way back to 1921, when research began with an emphasis on using drawings to determine intelligence levels. Cathy Malchiodi, in her

book *Understanding Children's Drawings*, writes in her first chapter on the history of analysis that this study "has quite a long tradition in the fields of psychiatry, psychology, art therapy and education. This long-standing fascination has generated a great deal of information on how children use drawing to express themselves, information that clinicians, counselors and teachers who use drawings with children should know." She also describes multidimensional approaches to understanding children's drawings and how important it has become to find additional ways of understanding children.

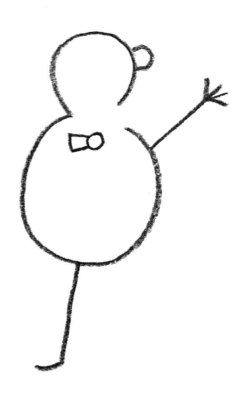

Drawing the human figure

In 1926 the "Draw-a-Man" test was developed, based on the assumption that certain capabilities of drawing indicated a child's intellectual development and could therefore be used as a measure of intelligence. Drawing the human figure became a popular subject of many studies during the first half of the 20th century, and intuitively analysts began to realize that drawings of human beings could provide information about the children themselves, as well as how children perceive others. In addition, specialists started to look at the drawings to help ascertain the child's development and personality.

Eventually the "Draw-a-Person" test became widely known and a major influence on almost all research on clinical applications of human figure drawings, including that of children, and it is still used today.

Emotional aspects

During the latter half of the 20th century, the idea began to take hold that drawings could also be used to determine the emotional and internal psychological states of the child. One of the drawing tests developed was the "House, Person, Tree" drawing because of the familiarity of these three themes for young children. Subsequently in her research, Audrey McAllen changed the order to "Person, House, Tree."

No consensus

Malchiodi writes that there is "no definite consensus about the meaning and purpose of art expressions and no singular, reliable way to interpret content." Children can express themselves in drawing and in other media such as modeling, painting, handwork and movement.

In this study I chose the modeling medium of beeswax to complement the drawing studies. I asked the children to model a self-portrait at the beginning of the third grade and again in January of the same year. The three-dimensional addition to the study added another aspect to studying the children's view of themselves.

The connection between the human being and her house and environment

Rudolf Steiner, the Austrian-born educator and philosopher, describes in some of his literature how the child, after having been enclosed in the womb up to the time of her birth, continues to have a protective life-giving "sheath" until about the seventh year. Michaela Strauss writes that many times children return again and again to drawing a ball of whirls, even at the age of having long outgrown this early phase of drawing. She likens this to adults' habits of sleeping in a curled-up ball in the embryonic position. The womb is the house that "shuts us in," that protects us from the world outside. In drawings, the house has a variety of environmental additions and accompaniments: an animal, flowers, a path, a swing, a fence, a pond. All the additional components accompanying the house have their own individual roles to play in the picture of the child's development.

Houses and other buildings

The archetypal house can appear very early in the form of whirls and other spherical, enclosing forms and shapes, such as a beehive or a dome-like form. Gradually the roundness acquires an angularity. The base of the house is often square or rectangular. In Rhoda Kellogg's research, the most commonly drawn combination of shapes by children ages five to eight years for a house is the square at the base, with a triangle for the roof.

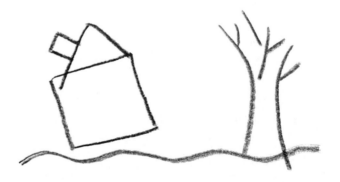

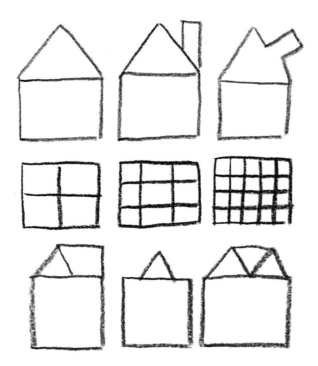

Buildings are constructed through drawing a combination of diagrams in a variety of ways. There are countless different designs and combinations.

Roofs

The roof appears as a triangle or a trapezoid. Sometimes the roof is shown with windows, square or round.

Chimneys

Chimneys are sometimes part of the roofline, at other times they are attached after the roofline is completed. A house can have more than one chimney. Smoke appears coming out of the chimney, often drawn as a swirling spiral.

Windows

Windows are primarily rectangular or square, sometimes round. They appear singly or in multiples. They can have a single cross or multiple crossed lines. The most dominant window design for children ages five to eight years is the square with one single cross.

Doors

Doors come in shapes of vertical rectangles, triangles or a vertical half circle. Handles on doors may appear in drawings by children as young as age three. The dominant door design is a vertical rectangle, with a door handle on the middle right side.

Animals

Children do not generally draw animals until about the age of five. The child's first efforts to draw animals look very like humans. Simple changes are required for the child to change a human shape to that of an animal. Some appear with the trunks in a horizontal or upright direction with ears coming out of the top of the head. By changing the position of the facial features in relation to the torso of the human, the child suggests the image of a horizontal animal.

Trees and flowers

Between the ages of five and seven, trees appear in many different varieties. The straight line and the curve are created with many varied combinations. The tops of the trees are a collection of suns, radials and mandalas, with straight lines making up the trunk.

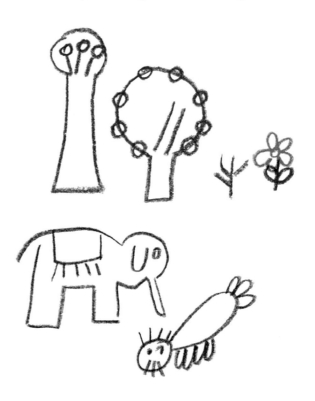

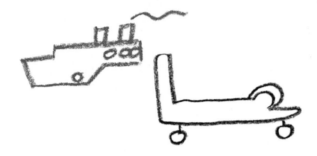

The first tree that appears can be seen as very similar to the human figure. It has a round head on top of a trunk and the treetop has many markings, such as circles or dots. Some trees take on the look of armless humans. Internal branches appear in addition to divided branches, without enclosing lines on the perimeter.

A frequent theme is trees drawn as Christmas art. Between the ages of five and seven, the child draws flowers, primarily with a single stem and with the images of suns and mandalas constituting the flower petals.

Boats, trains, planes and spaceships

Between the ages of five and eight, children are frequently absorbed by and drawn to objects that transport things from one place to another. Boats and planes often appear in drawings. The shapes children are able to produce at this stage are combinations of curves and straight lines with the circle and rectangle used most commonly. The shapes become increasingly complex as the child develops through the years.

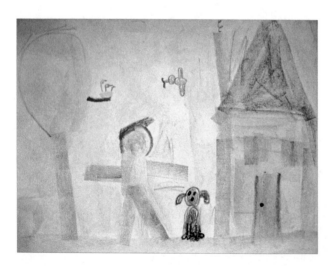

Ladders

Axes of symmetry are often found in a pair of straight lines running parallel to one another, with straight short lines crossing the two vertical lines—as struts in a ladder. The ladder can be compared to a rib cage created in picture form. The ladders are a recurring and favorite theme of children and often appear in the "Person, House, Tree" pictures. The verticality of the ladder and the horizontal lines crossing it indicate the human being standing in space. Strauss refers to this phenomenon in drawing as the child's showing its skeleton, its architecture.

Fences

Fences can appear as early as five years of age and can surround the house or extend from the house on the left and right sides. The fence is usually shown as a series of vertical lines with one, two or three horizontal continuous lines running along the top half or through the middle.

Swings

Swings appear most often hung from trees. Sometimes they are empty of figures and other times they are occupied.

Ponds and rivers

Ponds and rivers appear between the ages of six and eight and can also appear in older children's drawings. A pond can be shown with one or several ducks or other waterfowl, or with a person fishing. Rivers appear with or without bridges.

Islands

Islands do not usually appear until the age of twelve to thirteen and can indicate the onset of puberty.

"Person, House, Tree" drawings: what they can tell us

Audrey McAllen began her work with children initially with those who had learning difficulties. After a time of study, she decided to use the "Person, House, Tree" drawing as a tool and a support for understanding the child. She found, to her astonishment, that students as old as eleven years were producing drawings with houses floating on the page. Trees had spindly branches or wide, heavy trunks, with a ball shape for the foliage. She gradually became aware that these drawings could give the teacher an objective view of the physical structure and growth of the child.

The exercises

McAllen devised a movement sequence exercise to be carried out before beginning the drawing. The process of jumping, clapping and counting takes about two minutes. The exercise was designed to bring the whole body into movement, to "connect the body to all spatial dimensions, to challenge the will, to deepen the breathing, and enliven the circulation." (McAllen, *Reading Children's Drawings*) The resulting drawings contain the archetype of the human structure and form of the body as the child experiences them. The mediator of this imprinting is the jumping-induced deepening of breathing that activates the cerebral spinal fluid. McAllen recognized the objectivity of drawings after her students had done the movement and counting sequence, and later discovered that neurological research bore out her theory.

Rudolf Steiner's philosophy

McAllen's work and research is based largely on Rudolf Steiner's view of the human being. His philosophy holds that the human being is four-fold, with a physical body, a life force, a soul force and an ego. The physical body, along with the three other forces, develops as the child grows from birth to adulthood and gains a foothold at different stages of the child's development.

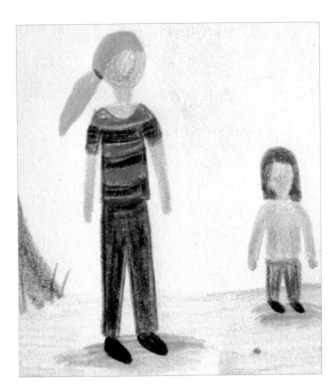

Three archetypes

McAllen saw the three archetypes of Person, House and Tree as fundamental indicators of the overall picture of the child's development of body geography, spatial orientation and sidedness. She writes that the details belonging to the *house*, such as the windows, door, chimney and path, show body geography that the soul has built up during the first seven years of the child's life. The *person* gives the idea of the growth of the soul powers in building up the body that should be ready for learning activities after the change of teeth. The *tree* is described as "the life-line," the picture of the breathing system and the nervous system.

Drawings as a tool

As a remedial specialist, McAllen uses drawings as a tool to help understand children who have learning difficulties. She makes a clear distinction between the child's school readiness, as indicated by the structural development completion of the physical body and its constitutional aspects, and the realm of the psychological. She emphasizes that the psychological aspect, as indicated at times by the use of colors, be left to the class teacher.

The class teacher's role

For the classroom teacher, all the children's drawings can be a valuable tool for understanding where they are in their structural/physical development, as well as the state of their souls. Each child has her own story to tell, and each child's story is unique. Children may have social difficulties and be otherwise extremely capable. They may have challenges in the classroom relating to their temperament or shyness, and yet be free and easy on the playground.

Children may have older siblings who have an effect on them that causes them to act in certain ways, either in the classroom or on the playground. Some children have extraordinary family circumstances or are adopted from different cultures. Some children may not have had all the opportunities to develop their physical bodies in their early childhood years. They may not have had the necessary stimulation for movement or the fostering and nurturing of emotional attachments and bonds so crucial to their well-being.

No child is alike unto another, and drawings truly reflect this in a wonderful way. The children have much to tell their teachers, and drawings are an easily accessible tool for personal understanding and support of the child.

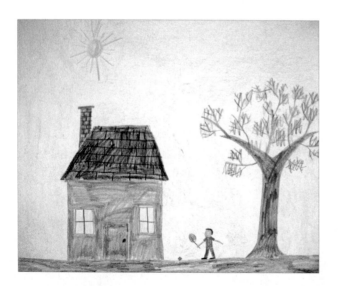

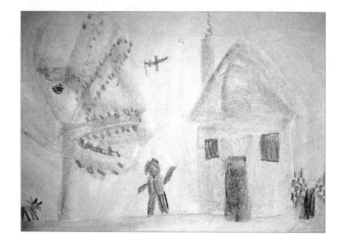

What the drawings of a seven-year-old can tell us: what to look for

Drawings can show that the child has completed the birth-to-seven development or whether one or the other stage has not yet been completed. Drawings can show lack of spatial orientation. Certain elements can be missing, such as a house, a tree or a person. Drawings can also show the figure as undeveloped, as in drawings done by three- and four-year-olds. There are many aspects of the elements in a drawing that can be viewed and studied.

Spatial orientation

Spatial orientation is how the child experiences and relates to the space around her: the front, the back, sides, above and below. Are the elements in the drawing on the ground or are they floating in the air? Is there a sky above and an earth below?

Person-body geography

The drawing of the archetypal human being indicates how the child feels in her own body and where she is in the process of development of body geography awareness. Children draw human beings parallel to their own development.

It takes up to the seventh year to develop body geography, that they have an awareness of and can point to their various body parts. The human being in their drawings should at this time have all the body parts present: head, neck, trunk, arms and hands, legs and feet. Children may draw persons without feet or hands, a figure without a waist and neck. The arms may protrude from the middle chest area, instead of protruding from the shoulders. Moreover, a person can be drawn as a stick figure, showing no thickness to the body.

If some of the body parts are missing, or the limbs are drawn in an uneven or stilted way, McAllen suggests "there may be some hidden structural compression to the natural function of the nervous system, affecting coordination and other bodily skills. This may lead to lack of integration of the vestibular system (sense of balance) and proprioception (sense of movement)."

Birth history

McAllen recommends the teacher ask the parents about the birth history of the child: the details of the birth itself, how the child cried and whether there was any inexplicable crying during the first months of life. If the child has a complicated birth history, McAllen suggests seeking help in the form of cranio-sacral osteopathy to rule out or treat any possible misalignment of cranial bones and spinal structure.

Reasons for distortions

There are other reasons for distortions in figure drawings, such as accidents in the early years or sudden, unexpected falls or banging of the head. The child's history of birth to school age can be helpful information as part of the analysis of a child's drawings.

House

The house has several aspects that are a very important part of assessing how the child feels in her body. Questions to ask are: Does the house have windows? How many are there, what shape are they and do they have crosses or curtains? Is there a chimney on the roof and how is it situated on the roof? What is the shape of the roof? Is the house "archetypal," consisting of a rectangle or square with a triangle roof, separated from the square by a line?

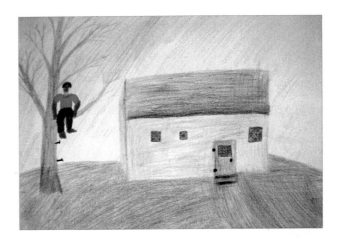

The base square represents the physical/earthly body of the child, and the triangle as a roof on the top of the square as the soul/spiritual aspect. The windows represent the soul looking out towards the world. The crossings over the windows indicate the child is protected from the world. The door indicates a way in and out of the body, especially when there is a doorknob. The chimney signifies the will forces at work in the body.

Tree

The tree indicates the breathing/feeling aspect of the child's stage of development. The tree of life is in us, and is pictured in our trachea, bronchi, and lungs, but upside down. Aspects to look for are the height of the tree, the proportion between the trunk and the branches, the roots, branches and the leaves. Analysis of trees can indicate asthma, congestion or other respiratory problems, the nature of the child's soul, and the nerve-sense activity. Both breathing and sensing connect us to the world around us. In early child development, the fir tree is a favorite theme.

Additional themes

Children may add some items to their "Person, House, Tree" drawings, though they often choose not to. Whether extra elements are added to the drawing depends largely on the child's development, her interest in the world, and how much initiative she has. Some children show recurring themes such as the family dog, a shovel in the hand, a swing hanging from the tree. Occasionally a river, a stream or a

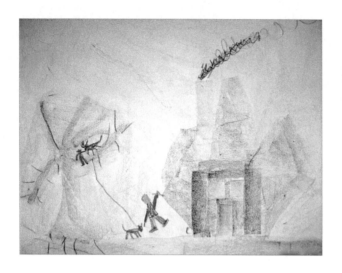

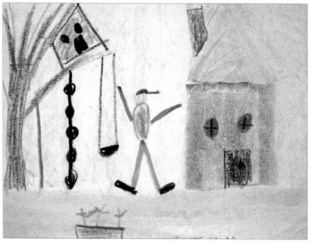

pond appears. Other figures may join the person, sometimes a whole family. Details around the house such as paths, driveways, parking lots and cars are other possible additions.

Colors

From years of observing children, McAllen found that the colors they choose in their drawings call attention to aspects of their soul life. She relates how certain soul conditions can be challenging—such as the egoistic qualities of greed and jealousy or needs arising from family situations and circumstances. Sometimes there may be a need for medical help or artistic therapy.

For further insights and information, please read Audrey McAllen's books: *Reading Children's Drawings* and *The Extra Lesson.*

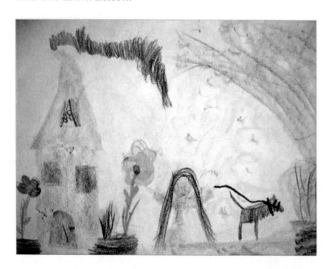

The "Person, House, Tree" drawings over the eight years

The assignment of the "Person, House, Tree" drawing at the beginning, middle and end of the year became a highlight for my class. Students looked forward to the activity and at times anticipated the event, even asking for it. They would wait eagerly while the paper was being distributed, and they knew it was a drawing they would not keep but freely give away to the teacher. Typically they were able to complete the drawing in forty-five minutes, though some children always needed more time. Much to my amazement their enthusiasm continued through eighth grade.

Practical considerations

The size of the drawing paper became smaller as the students got older, due to changing from drawing with beeswax blocks and sticks in the earlier grades to drawing with colored pencils in later years. The movement exercise that preceded the assignment was easy enough to include in the early years when the students naturally imitated the teacher. However, from about fourth grade on up, the exercises needed explanation to increasingly maturing students, and a few jumping jack movements before the drawing had to suffice.

Observations

It is best not to make it obvious that you are observing the students while drawing. Some children can get very self-conscious. I found it most interesting that not even one of the students ever looked to see what the others were doing. They were mostly absorbed in their own work and did not have to be separated more than the usual spaces between the desks.

Recurring themes

One of the recurring themes that stood out was of the child sitting up in a tree, even in later years. Another recurring theme, beginning in first grade and repeated all through the grades, was that of flowers bathed in sunlight with fruit on the branches of trees.

Another recurring theme was action, such as playing with a ball or working in the yard. Only in the later grades, beginning around fourth grade, will the children begin to depict movement in the figure. Until then, the figures are standing still and mostly seen from the front and a few from the side.

Imagination

One of the most interesting things I observed was that the students' drawings became more imaginative as they grew older and progressed into middle school. Houses became more fantastical and landscapes more varied. Some students tried to depict their own houses. Others clearly imagined or remembered places they had been to, had read about or were studying.

Development and style

Observing how children develop over the years, watching their styles of drawing emerge, is highly rewarding. To gain an insight into their soul life and their imagination is a real asset to the teacher. Most of all, it is a joy to have the possibility to look into their world and try to understand their unique personalities and temperaments. Style mysteriously begins to develop early on and matures gradually. It is possible after some years to begin to identify each student's style and to ascertain their individual temperaments as revealed through their drawings.

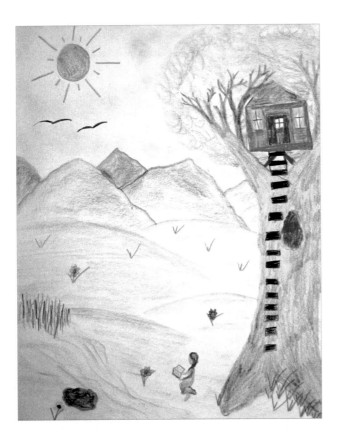

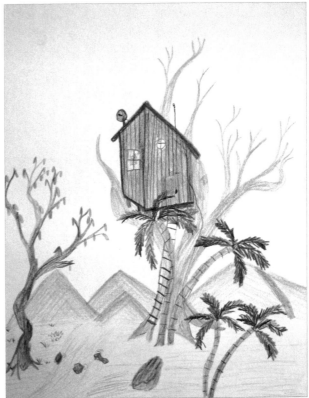

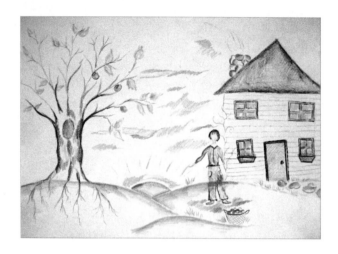

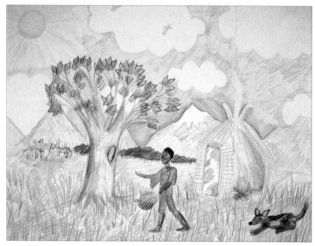

The temperaments

It is fascinating to observe the outward manifestations of children's temperaments and then to see whether this correlates or not to what they express in their drawings. At times it can be surprising. The most melancholic child can create the most sunny drawings! Often the temperament remains hidden and may be more easily observed in the child's actions and words, rather than in drawings.

I cannot rest, I must draw, however poor the result, and when I have a bad time come over me, it is a stronger desire than ever.

– Beatrix Potter

Self-taught art and the influence of the teacher

Children "teach" themselves to draw. This begins with the very first imprint around the age of two when the child is able to grasp a chalk or crayon. This process of self-teaching parallels the child's learning to make shapes in the sand on the beach or in the sandbox, or picking up a paintbrush and painting with paint. Children find their way gradually to the representation of the human figure, animals, and the world around them. Textures, as well as light and shade, for the most part, do not appear in self-taught art in the beginning.

Influence of the teacher

Teachers can have a decisive influence on the development of children's art. Rhoda Kellogg puts great emphasis on how important it is for children to develop their art unhindered by adults. She emphasizes that children are self-taught and should not be interfered with in their development of drawing.

Sylvia Fein also mentions how teachers can be destructive to the process of children's gradually acquiring detail and complexity in their drawings. She gives the example of a teacher, who, knowing that five-year-old children use circles to construct human and animal figures, drew a giraffe on the blackboard composed entirely of multiple circles and asked the children to copy it. The resulting drawings showed

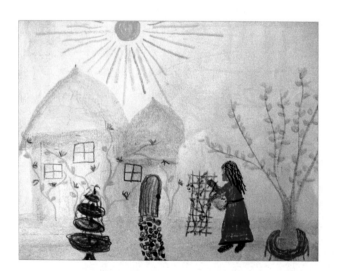

that one child had tried to do what the teacher asked for and no more, whereas the drawing she had done at home showed her ability beyond the simplistic use of circles. Her "natural drawing, perfectly formed and freed by the absence of instructions, includes her organized observations from trips to the zoo."

In my classroom experience, however, a teacher can have a beneficial influence on a child's drawing without compromising the child's personal style, spontaneous creativity or enthusiasm.

The teacher as a guide

The influence of a teacher should come at a time when children are ready to enter first grade and move beyond the drawing of linear shapes. By third grade the child wants to depict the world around her as she sees it in reality. Shapes of humans and animals are not hollow with lines around them; they are solid shapes that have a front, sides and a back. Many children, if left to their own development in drawing after the age of seven, do not move beyond the linear, cartoon-type drawings. Frustration can set in, as the linear representations do not satisfy the child and she can give up and avoid drawing altogether. Children can be guided. They do not need to wait for art instruction in the middle school years or high school.

Children also need guidance in learning about proportions and gestures. The guidance can begin in a gentle, age-appropriate way as early as first grade, to gradually prepare the way for the middle school years.

A three-dimensional effect

The teacher can guide the children towards drawing with a three-dimensional effect by setting the stage for drawing with tones. Children can be shown how to draw with tone and color, rather than outlining a form that is either filled in or left empty.

Many adults never develop their own art beyond the linear outline approach. But working anew with form and color, devoid of the tyranny of the outline, can create new possibilities for art and expression. This can be a breakthrough for adults and awaken new artistic possibilities and directions.

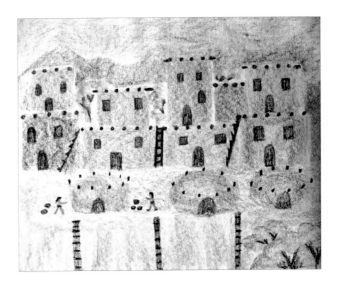

Working in a similar way with children before and around the age of nine can help them move beyond self-taught art towards artistic representations of the three-dimensional world around them. It can help them realize that working with form through tone and color is possible for everyone, and that the representation of forms found in the "real" world does not always depend on exact linear contours and details.

The aesthetic quality of a drawing

The teacher can also influence the quality of a child's drawing by gently showing possibilities of taking greater care in applying tones instead of rushing the drawing. Many children take great care over the active components of the drawing, and then rush with the background. They can be guided into seeing that a background, or the setting of the scene, has equal importance to the drawing in its entirety and overall aesthetic appearance.

Gesture and movement
as seen through self-portraits

*Child art integrates movement and vision, the perception of overall shapes
and the perception of details, familiar line formations and new ones, stimulation and reaction,
aesthetic pleasure and muscular satisfaction.*

- Rhoda Kellogg

Each child's drawing is unique and can be very revealing. This is particularly apparent when we look at the self-portraits. Much can be gleaned about the child's growth and development from the gesture of the portrait and its relationship to movement.

The first three years of school are a period which may be considered psychologically as a unit. Bernard Lievegoed writes in his book, *Phases of Childhood*, "It is a particularly happy period. Everything conspires to place the child in a state of balance and harmony. The awakening forces of the will are still greatly influenced by the imagination and eagerly reach out into an expanding world of thought. A whole new world opens up and the child surrenders to the world with awe." This sense of awe is expressed in the arms reaching out and upwards. The child shows a gesture of openness to the world that is trusting and eager.

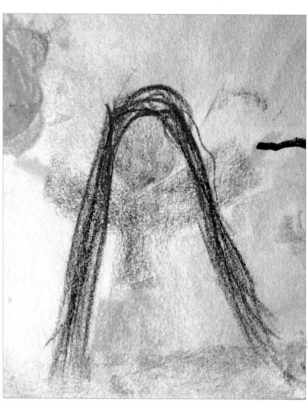

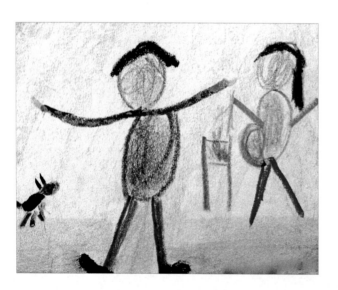

Ages 7 through 11

For the seven-year-old, Lievegoed says, "images are not yet sharply defined; they are fluid, mobile and active like people in a stage play." The drawings reflect dreaminess and a lack of self-consciousness. They also reflect an as yet undeveloped capacity to show movement of the body. The seven- to nine-year-old is not yet ready to master the complexity of leg movement. Legs are portrayed as straight down and frequently drawn with a frontal view. The arms drawn in an upright gesture are shown straight up

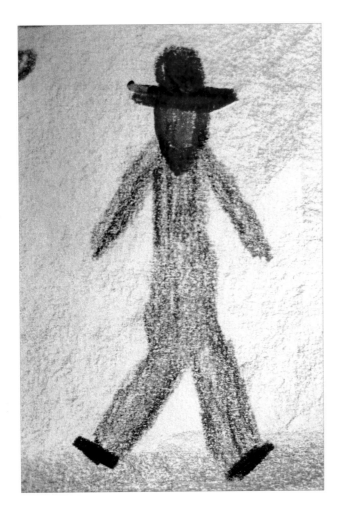

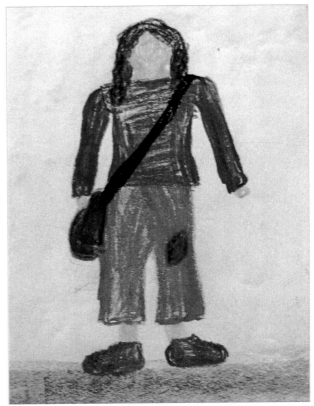

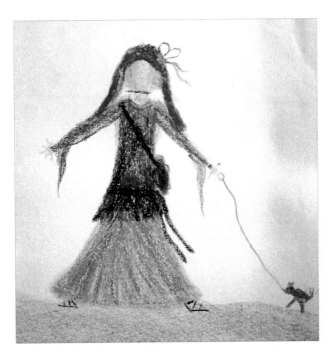

and often symmetrical. The "stiffness" of the figures also reflects an as yet undeveloped consciousness of movement. Movement is a natural part of a child's daily life and an intrinsic part of being. The child does not think about running—she just runs.

In the nine-year-old "a complete change seems to have come over his feelings, as though he has lost the protection of the imaginative world projected outside himself, as though suddenly he experiences the world as a hostile place." (Lievegoed) While any sign of movement is still more or less absent from the legs, the gesture of the arms changes. For the most part, by third grade the gesture of the arms is downwards and they are no longer open and outstretched. Girls in particular turn more inward and show the arms along the side of the body in a less active and more resting, natural position. You can think of the descent of the arms as a gesture of protection from the outside world. You can also see details appearing, such as hair ribbons, hats, and bags slung over a shoulder. The view continues to be frontal, and the legs are usually portrayed straight down.

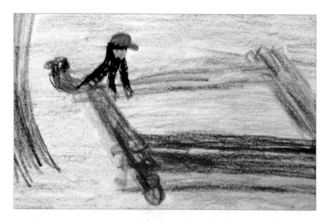

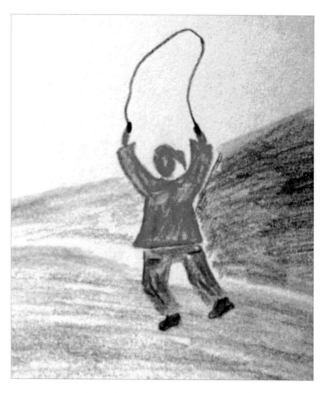

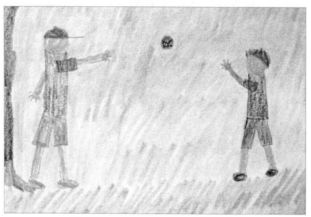

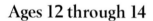

Ages 12 through 14

At this stage the child gains a new relationship to the world around her. This new relationship brings increased self-consciousness and is reflected in the drawings in several ways. Boys are more apt to show themselves dressed for sports and are usually actively engaged, on their own or with a peer. Even though the boys are playing, the legs are still often portrayed as stationary, while the arms are clearly outstretched (albeit appearing fairly awkward). The ability to show running legs begins to appear from around age twelve onwards. Ironically this is the age when movement often begins to become more sluggish, as opposed to the young child's endless need for running around.

Children tend to show movements from a side view, which helps the child articulate movement gestures more readily. Showing movement gesture is a formidable achievement for the growing and developing student. Girls show an interest in the way they look and dress, portraying themselves in

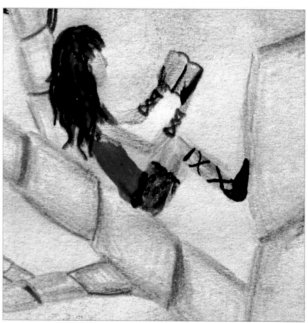

stationary positions, such as in reading a book up in a tree, or in movement, such as jumping rope.

By the time students are in middle school, many of them can portray themselves in a well-articulated manner. The body is well proportioned, and a lot of detail is added to the portrait. Patterns appear,

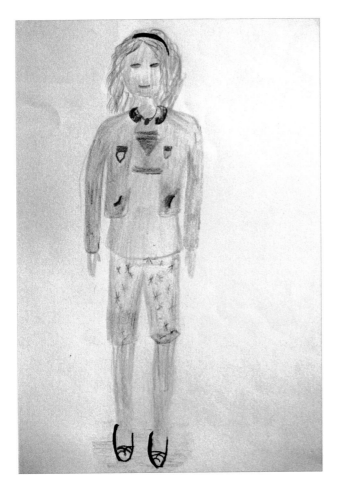

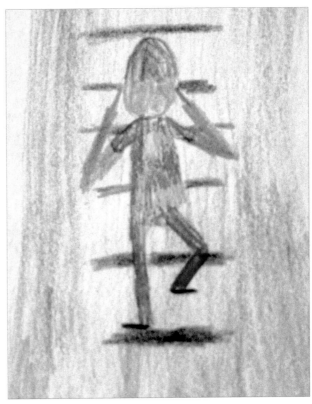

as well as pockets, necklaces and shoelaces. Some of the self-portraits show a remarkable youthfulness, in particular those of the boys. One boy portrays himself in the sandbox, another sits up on a tree branch and a third climbs a ladder up to a tree fort—all engaged in purposeful, physical activities typical of the younger child.

At times a portrait from this age can clearly show the lack of differentiation and articulation in the figure, even though there is a valiant attempt to show the movement of climbing up a ladder. There is no foreshortening of the legs, and the hands are barely holding on to the rungs. It is clear that portraying movement is a most formidable challenge for the student in the elementary grades.

The portrait of the "young at heart" may or may not indicate a corresponding lack of maturity in mental processes. Self-portraits are a fascinating insight into a child's development and growth, but as such there is no "cookie cutter" formula for each stage or for interpretation.

Modeling self-portraits in beeswax

An equally fascinating insight into child development can be gained from having students model their self-portraits in beeswax. The relationship between their ability to model themselves and to draw their own portraits would make for a very interesting study. The following illustrations show three portraits from third grade.

The first one has the arms still upwards with a large head and upper trunk, small legs and no feet. The arms are extended out of the middle part of the trunk rather than the shoulders. The second illustration shows another boy, this time on a skateboard. The emphasis is on the legs and feet and the skateboard underneath. The legs are spread out and the body looks ready for action. The arms are spread out sideways as if for balance and the hands are missing. The third illustration shows a girl with clearly articulated hands and feet. She is well proportioned with arms down at her side, and the details of two pigtails and polka dots on her skirt.

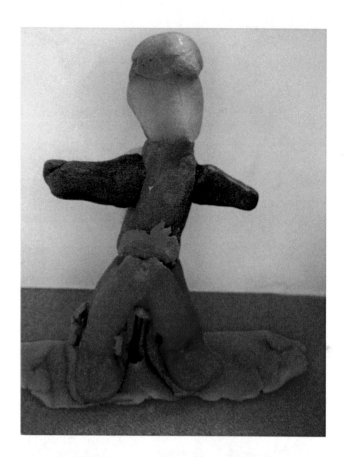

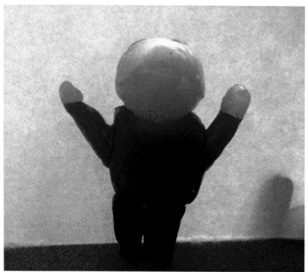

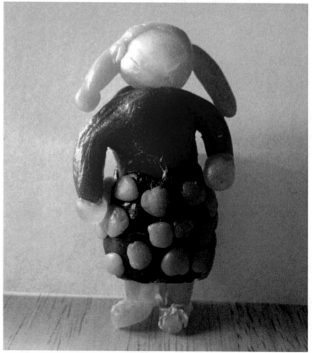

Daily drawing is key in the lives of our children
Promoting reflective practice
by Helen-Ann Ireland

Drawing is an everyday event in the Waldorf classroom. Following the advice of Rudolf Steiner, teachers incorporate time for students to draw in their main lesson books during the morning block. These drawings illustrate the theme of the main lessons and are directly connected to the lesson. In first grade, the fairy tales and number gnomes, and in eighth grade, science demonstrations, maps, and portraits of famous historical figures are a few of the topics rendered. The reasons for this are multi-layered. There are specific artistic skills to be learned, habits of mind to be developed, specific instructional points to be made and reflective practice to be developed. All of these are part of what helps a child to know a subject, otherwise known as the act of cognition.

Drawing techniques

Drawing serves a very specific purpose in Waldorf classrooms. First, there are drawing skills that teachers expect children to develop over the course of their eight years. Children learn to draw forms using color; they learn to develop a composition on the page; they learn perspective using color and placement of objects. As they mature, they learn to draw from nature and the objects around them. Over time, they are exposed to various drawing techniques as they learn to use different kinds of drawing tools—beeswax crayons, colored pencils, pastels and ink.

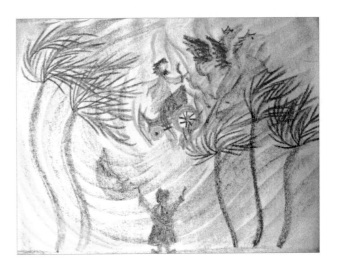

Educating the aesthetic sensibility

In addition to teaching the techniques of drawing, the teacher is educating the child's aesthetic sense. The child learns how colors work together, which ones are complementary, which ones are supplementary, and how to work with these to mix and make gradations between them. This helps the child develop creativity using color, which is the basis from which other kinds of creativity can flow.

Using drawing for academic instruction

There are very specific instructional reasons for the pictures that the teachers work with. For the youngest children, the teacher guides the subject matter of the drawing to illustrate the denouement of the story that the children will be writing about following their drawing. Or the teacher chooses a scene from the story to be able to write something that illustrates the sounds of *ea* in a variety of words

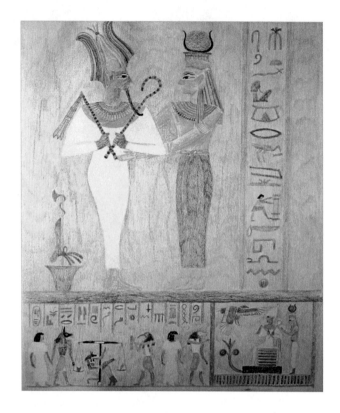

(*bread, break, beak*, for example). As the children mature, they may draw three scenes from Roman history that show the key points of the history lesson as they emerge through the teacher's storytelling or, in science lessons, the lab equipment used for a science demonstration. These drawings are always created in full color so that the student has a lively engagement with the topic, which can enhance their memory of the lesson. Berry's study in 1991 found that "all forms of color are better than black and white for recall."

Drawing as a time for reflection

Steiner was adamant about the role of the arts in education, and today there are many scholars who support these ideas. Besides making the invisible realm of the imagination visible on the page, the person drawing is creating another kind of knowledge through the activity of drawing. Drawing gives the student time to reflect upon the subject matter. As Daniel Goleman has described, there is an incubation period before a person can have the "aha" experience. Drawing provides this incubation space in the students' day. It gives them time for quiet, personal reflection on the main lesson topic. This is

a crucial moment in the child's learning. Drawing provides time for the children to synthesize the lesson material, to make connections to other learning and to deepen their connection with the material presented by the teacher. Therefore, drawing can be seen as an aid to developing the child's cognition. In his book, *The Unschooled Mind*, Howard Gardner recommends that students have an aesthetic experience as one of the pathways to understanding a topic.

Developing habits of mind

Eliot Eisner has championed using the arts to engage students in their learning. He asserts that "in learning to engage in that process [visual arts], perception is refined, imagination stimulated, judgment fostered, and technical skills developed." (Eisner, p. 15) Lois Hetland and Ellen Winner, et al., speak eloquently in their book, *Studio Thinking*, about the habits of mind that are created in the artist's studio. They list seven habits of mind that are developed through the engagements of the visual arts. These "dispositions are used in academic arenas and in daily life: ....Observation, Envisioning, Reflecting, Expressing, Exploring, Engaging and Persisting, and Understanding." (Hetland, et al., p. 7) Eric Jensen has also made a case for the visual arts and linked them to better cognitive ability. Using Davidson's study in 1996, Jensen points out that for a group of third graders he studied, "drawing enabled them to clarify

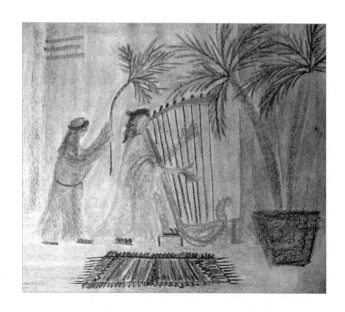

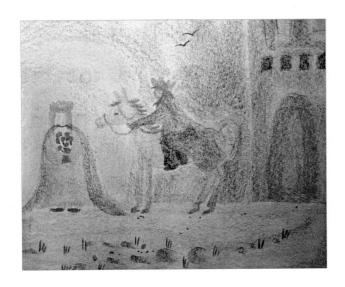

their ideas better, which improved comprehension and clarity." (Jensen, p. 59)

If we, as educators, have the goal of teaching for understanding, then drawing is one of the important avenues for student engagement with curriculum material. Because the students are drawing from the main lesson stories, they are making a direct connection to the material through the power of their will. This engagement provides the opportunity for the student to reflect on the material being presented. Donald Schön coined the term "reflection in action" as a way for individual adults to learn from their experiences in life. Applying this to children, drawing provides a way for them to reflect on what they are learning—to make a personal connection to it.

Ultimately, the purpose of daily drawing in full color is to awaken the child's aesthetic and creative self. These techniques and the benefits of daily drawing are not only for use in Waldorf classrooms. They can be applied in any classroom in any school setting to enhance the creative process. There are many scholars who have identified the kinds of minds that will be needed in the future. They assert that, rather than trying to fit students into the existing world, the capacity for creative thinking will become a necessary quality that human beings will need to be able to solve world problems. In his book, *A Whole New Mind*, Daniel Pink gives a thoughtful look at what he calls "the cultural creatives" who will drive the inventions of the future and why this is necessary.

Drawing is one of the pathways for learning and for fostering creativity. It is not just fluff. It has an important function in children's learning experience that can enhance cognition—their process of knowing. This applies to children in any educational setting.

References

Berry, L.H. (1991). "Visual complexity and the pictorial memory: A fifteen year research perspective." Paper presented at the annual meeting of the Association for Educational Communications and Technology (Eric Document Reproduction Service No. ED 334947).

Eisner, E.W. (2002). *The Arts and the Creation of Mind*. New Haven: Yale University Press.

Gardner, H. (1991). *The Unschooled Mind: How Children Think and How Schools Should Teach*. New York: BasicBooks.

Gazzaniga, M. (2008). Dana Consortium report on arts and cognition. "Learning, arts, and the brain." New York/Washington, DC: Dana Press.

Goleman, D. (2011). The a-ha moment. http://www.youtube.com/embed/fZmTY8d9Jy4?autoplay=1&hd=1.

Hetland, L. et al. (2007). *Studio Thinking: The Real Benefits of Visual Arts in Education*; Teacher's College Press, NY and London.

Jensen, E. (2001). *Arts with the Brain in Mind*, ASCD; Alexandria, VA.

Langer, E.J. (1989). *Mindfulness*. Reading, MA: Addison-Wesley Pub. Co.

Pink, D.H. (2006). *A Whole New Mind: Why Right-brainers Will Rule the Future*. New York: Riverhead Books.

Schön, D.A. (1983). *The Reflective Practitioner: How Professionals Think in Action*. New York: BasicBooks.

Helen-Ann Ireland was a Waldorf classroom teacher for twenty years in two different schools—Honolulu Waldorf School in Hawaii and Pine Hill Waldorf School in New Hampshire. She is now pursuing doctoral studies in Educational Leadership K-12 at UMass/Amherst. She lives in Wilton with her husband, who likes to paddle around the oceans and lakes of New England.

Reflections from students

If we master a bit of drawing, everything else is possible.
– Alberto Giacometti

It is evident that in the early years most children really love to draw. They draw freely and unconsciously up to around the age of nine, after which drawing becomes an increasingly conscious activity. If the teacher is fortunate enough to be able to follow the students' progress over a number of years, the change of consciousness becomes apparent in varying degrees.

Some students will express their feelings easily and directly, while others are reluctant to show their emotions. Once they are in high school, and have gained some perspective on their elementary school experience, students become capable of reflecting on their time spent in the classroom.

The artwork

All the illustrations shown here, varying from still-lifes and portraits to science posters, are from high school students who graduated from eighth grade at Pine Hill Waldorf School in 2011. It is gratifying to see how the students have progressed in their skills and how several of them have pursued art in the high school years. Some day in the future there may be a chance to do another survey, once all the students are in or well beyond college.

Rounding out the classroom experience

A survey was sent out to students from the class of 2011 in their sophomore year to ascertain their reflections after a couple of years in high school. The questions were sent mostly to students who had been in the class since the early years. A second survey

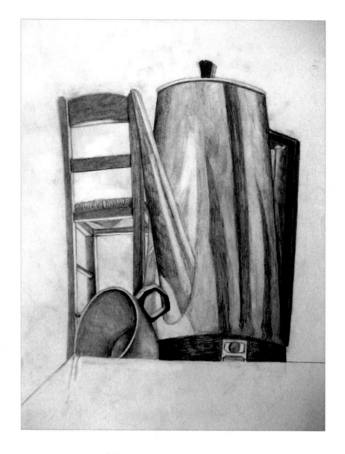

was sent out halfway through their senior year with questions pertaining to their last year of high school.

Ultimately the most important criteria are whether the students felt prepared for their high school experience and whether they gained enough confidence in the elementary grades. Just as they had been given a foundation in writing, they were also given the foundation to take their artistic skills to new levels in high school and beyond. Many of them have taken additional art courses.

The responses

The answers to the questions are varied, revealing and honest, none of them surprising, most of them positive. For the teachers who read this book, it may be helpful to see the questions and the answers, some of which are sprinkled throughout the chapters as quotes. It may aid the teacher in the awareness of what is important for young students and especially what is important in the critical middle school years.

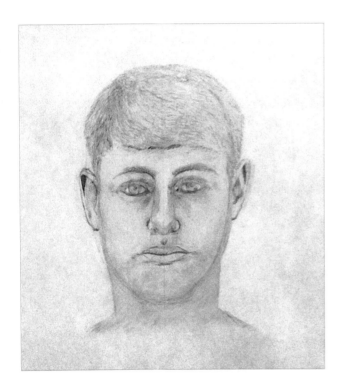

Sophomore year survey

What memories do you have of drawing in the classroom in the early years?

What I remember most about first through third grade are the form drawings which were fun to draw and make up on your own.

I remember how much the block crayons irritated, but now I kind of miss them. I remember drawing scenes from our stories and letters. I remember the saints and all the stories from our second grade play. My favorite was the fox and the crow.

I remember the "Person, House, Tree" drawings quite fondly.

I remember the "Person, House, Tree" drawings every year and doing a lot of forms and patterns.

I remember clearly trying to make my gnome hats fold to the side, and not understanding how they did. I also remember that I used common shapes to help me draw. Simple things like a head would be a circle, triangle for a dress or body and a square for pants and shirt.

I remember drawing the stories we would hear about during main lesson.

Would you have enjoyed school less had there been no main lesson book drawing, only writing?

Yes, the drawing was what made the writing bearable.

Yes, I would have enjoyed it less. I love drawing, and it brightened my day when I was able to illustrate my book.

Yes, the drawings were sometimes my favorite part of the main lesson book. My favorite was a Norse myth double-spread drawing of Ragnarok.

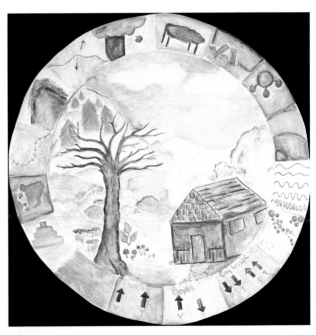

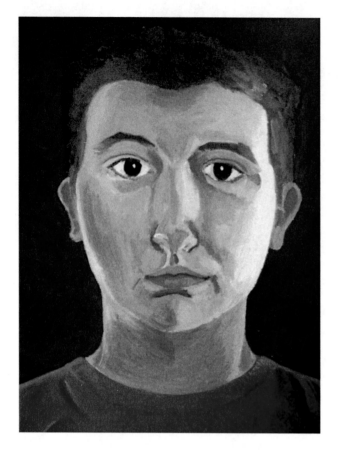

I enjoyed drawing the most when we learned the slant line technique, and in grade seven I remember doing a lot of maps—that was fun.

When we learned slant line and shading techniques. I also enjoyed our still-lifes and our eighth grade painting.

I think it was in sixth grade when we studied the countries in Europe, and I really enjoyed drawing all the little characteristics: foods, agricultural products and other goods from the countries.

Do you remember any time of frustration as regards drawing?

My only frustration then and now is drawing people, which is still the most frustrating part of drawing. Because it is hard to get the form of human beings correct.

I struggled with wet-on-wet watercolor, I loaded my brush too much and the paint would bleed.

I would have. I believe drawing embellishes a main lesson book and enriches it, and even now in sophomore social studies, my notebook is filled with (relevant) drawings!

Yes! Drawing was the best part!

Absolutely. Without drawing I would have found sitting and only writing extremely difficult.

Were there any times during the years when you enjoyed drawing the most?

I liked drawing a lot when we began to draw with pencils. It seemed to make it easier than drawing with blocks.

I really enjoyed drawing when it was more free in second through fourth grade when I didn't worry about buildings and such.

My favorite drawing year was definitely drawing the Roman people in sixth grade.

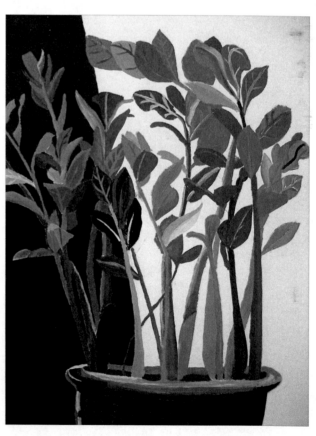

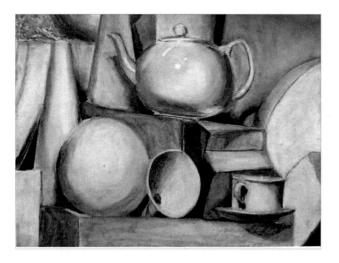

Slant line drawing was probably the most frustrating for me. It took a lot of time and thought, and by the end my hand hurt and I didn't enjoy how it looked.

I would always have a hard time slowing down and taking my time.

I always had a hard time drawing realistic animals with the right proportions.

Yes, all the time. I always get frustrated when it comes to drawing. I always remember this one time in second grade. I was drawing a person. A girl came up to me and said, "Why do your people's arms come from their hips?" Apparently I didn't know the placement of arms back then. This really frustrated me and put a bit of discouragement in my head.

What was your favorite drawing experience?

I loved drawing landscapes and plants during botany. I like drawing detailed objects or scenes. I'm pretty good at observing detail.

Most of the drawings I did in eighth grade were my favorite, especially portraits of famous people.

My favorite drawing experience was the pastel still-life of the fruits, bowl and cloth. It was centered on the page, accurately drawn, and I was happy with the results. I enjoyed pastels.

My favorite was always the main lesson book covers.

I absolutely loved drawing with the block crayons. I'm not sure if it counts here, but I think they were the best crayons ever invented. I still use the (now tiny) ones I still have!

Learning the different techniques we could use.

During the middle school years, what was your most important drawing lesson?

To slow down and take my time.

Shading from dark to light. This technique can be applied to many different mediums, can be used to define edges and shows perspective.

That a person is eight heads high. It wasn't something we spent time really practicing—it was mentioned a few times—but I have found it so useful!

In middle school, if I remember correctly, a big one was when we started out dark around the edges and faded to the center.

Perspective. I never really noticed perspective until it was introduced to me.

Probably learning to shade and how to draw things in perspective.

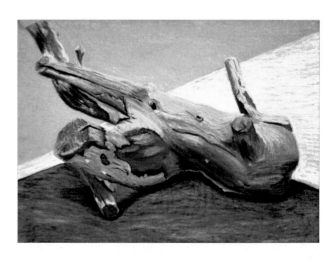

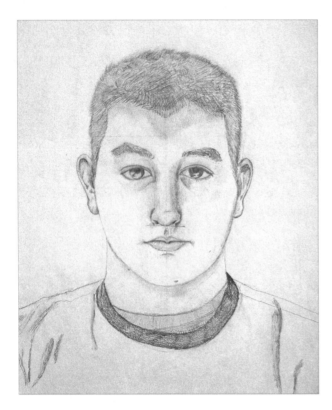

I gained a great structure for art through a strong foundation with mixing colors and drawing objects without lines.

I gained confidence from every drawing I did. The more practice I got, the more my confidence grew and allowed me to transform into a confident artist.

Yes, it has helped me in terms of creating a visual representation of my work in an organized, expressive way.

A lot. I may not be the best at all forms of art, but I always try it and hardly ever use an eraser, instead incorporating my mistakes into my artwork.

More confidence than most high school students have.

Have you applied your drawing skills while in high school?

I always use my shading skills. I love to shade; it is very helpful with all drawing.

Yes, very much.

Yes, I continue to use slant line, proportion knowledge, shading/light and shadow, polygons, portrait skills and composition knowledge in my artwork.

Yes, I do so all the time. Much of the time I'll use the style of having a person without a face if it is a picture for a younger child. It lets them decide what the people are feeling in the picture.

Yes, when we have to draw it helped. It also helped when I was in art class.

How much confidence did you gain from your elementary school art experience?

Some, though I don't feel very confident.

Do you still have imagination? How creative are you?

I like to draw and paint (watercolor and oil) in my free time (if I have free time).

I'm still creative.

I feel I am still very creative and definitely have imagination.

According to many of my teachers, creativity is my strong point and I am able to bring my imagination to every assignment, regardless of what class.

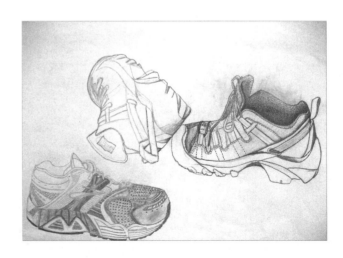

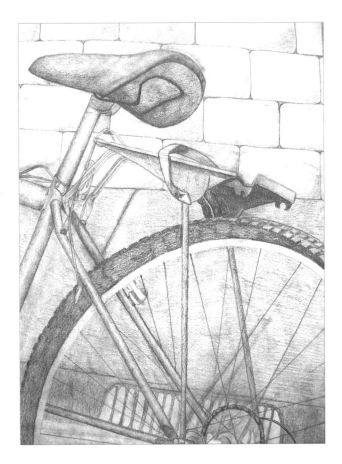

Somewhat in the beginning of freshman year, the class was asked to draw an ant. I was the only one in the class who had all the legs coming from the thorax.

Yes, it has helped in the way I perceive things.

It made me realize that things really aren't outlined, that the sky/other objects around them simply make it appear that way.

Can you think of anything missing from your drawing experience?

Nothing really.

Maybe more focus on drawing people in different positions.

Honestly, so far only one thing—Abstract. Steven is in my art class, and when abstract was the assignment, we both looked like two deer in the headlights.

I feel we went very in-depth in all techniques.

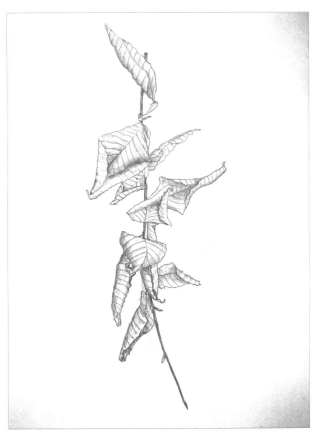

I like to think that I am very creative. I still sew dolls sometimes and am constantly drawing things from my mind.

Although I still draw, I am a big writer and musician now. I have sort of drifted away from drawing to writing.

Do you think that learning to draw objects and landscapes enhanced your knowledge of the world around you?

I learned to see the world in a different way than most people.

It made me look closer at my surroundings. My observation skills sharpened.

No, probably not, but it certainly helped with my drawings.

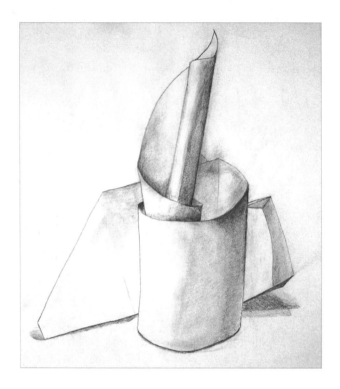

I think we should have been exposed to more different styles of art.

I wish we had done more drawing with graphite pencils.

Have you taken any art classes to further advance your skill level?

I have. I took an art class at the Currier Museum over the summer. It was called Portfolio Build.

I took a semester of visual arts freshman year.

Art 9, Art 10, painting styles, Art/Drawing/ Painting 1 and 2, pottery, clay sculpture, metal work, history through art.

Yes, about three over the past few years.

I have taken a lot. I even hope to have a career in an artistic field.

I took a photography class in ninth grade and a drawing class in tenth grade.

Do you feel you were well prepared for the high school art experience—did you have a good foundation of skills?

I definitely had a good foundation. I was well prepared and eased into the art classes.

I had a very good foundation, better than about 50% of the students in my grade.

Absolutely. My solid background prepared me for all projects in my art classes so far, even if the particular assignment has not been done before. Particular elements I had learned before made new, unfamiliar assignments easier to tackle.

I feel we had a great foundation that was much more in-depth and more advanced than that of my other classmates.

I really believe I did. A lot of what we speak about in high school I've either already done or already learned about, which has been very helpful!

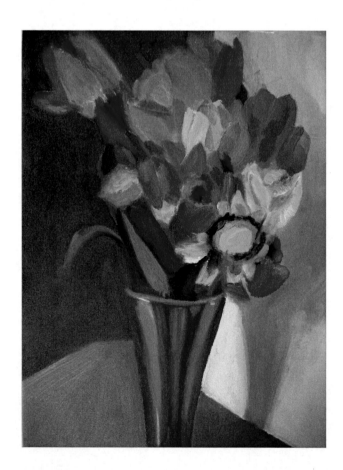

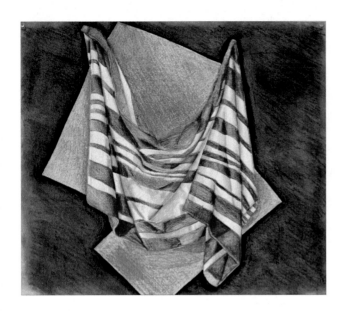

Senior year survey

How has your overall experience of art been during the high school years?

I have continued to put a lot of energy into art. But it has become more diverse for me. I have taken many different types of art classes and learned batik, pottery, oil painting, jewelry-making and sculpture. I wish I had all the time in the world to do art, but it is harder to keep my focus on art in high school. I have had a lot of academic classes, and in junior year especially, I didn't have one art class. But I have never forgotten it. This year I have been able to have a lot more time for it and I have missed it, but I love that this year I can get lost in art. High Mowing nurtures the creativity of the individual and I am extremely grateful for that.

My experience has been good, I haven't had as many opportunities to try new types of art throughout high school simply because my school offers only a limited amount of classes. However, there have been a lot of opportunities for me to incorporate art in my school work, such as projects, which has been nice.

It's been good, I've had multiple choices of art mediums, from painting and drawing to pottery and 3D art, and also media art such as photography and video.

Do you feel you were adequately prepared in your elementary grades to be able to succeed in high school art courses over the four years?

Most definitely. Having a teacher who is such an amazing artist was an incredible experience. I don't think any other school or teacher could have quite had such a positive impact on me as an artist.

I was definitely prepared, I was exposed to a lot of styles and techniques which was extremely helpful. I think the one thing I needed to practice more was observational drawing because that is something I tend to struggle with.

I took pottery this past year and feel like I was prepared for the molding and creating process. When I took drawing I also believe I had some basic skills that helped me. But when it came to the media art, I knew very little about it.

What arts courses, if any, are you taking this year?

Batik and Renaissance painting, pottery, art drawing and painting and jewelry.

This year I'm taking AP studio design and pottery.

I took pottery for a trimester, and I'm taking a year-long advanced film class.

How do you relate to or use your artistic skills in your other courses?

In every block class we have a lot of artistic aspects: block books, art projects, posters and such. When one has had much experience in the artistic world, it makes it easier to express oneself in other aspects. I see it in my writing, drama and many other things.

Many classes at Souhegan use projects and a lot of the projects involve decorating posters or coming up with ideas to show your work. I've found that I've used my art skills in creating the projects.

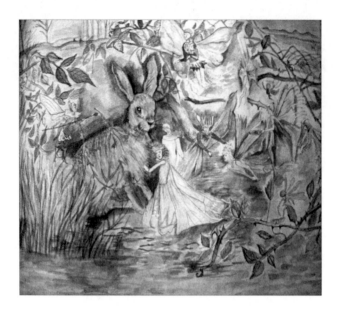

Typically in my other courses I have the chance to use art in projects. Up until junior year we had a new project almost every month and there was usually a way to show our knowledge through an art form. This year my classes have focused on papers and exams to prepare for college, so there hasn't been a chance to do any school work incorporating art.

How has your artistic foundation affected you in your high school years?

It has made me very prepared for almost every class. It is really helpful to have a strong foundation in creativity, as well as color-mixing and experience in a lot of mediums.

My artistic foundation has affected me well, I think without it I would have a very different perspective on things. I think, most of all, my artistic foundation has allowed me to think about things creatively.

It's helped steer me in the direction of what art classes I would want to take, but it's also helped me in other classes. Coming up with ideas and projects to express my work in class.

I don't think I would have become as invested with writing and film if I hadn't had the art I did in elementary and middle school. So it's affected my whole life ahead of me, as I'm going into film.

How do you think your artistry has shaped you as a person?

I am a very creative person and I really enjoyed doing art but if I hadn't gone to Pine Hill, it probably would have been overlooked, and I wouldn't be who I am today. I find release when I do art. I get stressed really easily, so for me to be able to relax while doing art is extremely valuable.

I think it has allowed me to explore different things in turn, enabling me to find the thing I'm interested in and shaping my perspectives.

How do you think your artistic sensibilities will serve you in the next four years and beyond?

I will always enjoy art and never stop doing it.

I think the biggest thing they provide is an attention to detail and more awareness in my surroundings.

I believe that I will continue to carry my artistic abilities and ideas through college to continue to help express my ideas and thoughts through what I'm doing with film.

What colleges are you applying to?

Reed, McGill, Sarah Lawrence, American University of Paris, Kenyon, Brandeis, Macalester.

Humboldt State University (and I got in!), Keene State, Colorado University Denver and New Hampshire Art Institute.

Chapman University, Loyola Marymount University, Emerson College, Savannah College of Art and Design, Champlain College, Syracuse University, Ithaca College, School of Visual Arts (NYC), Hampshire College, North Carolina School of Arts.

What connection, if any, does your foundation of arts have to do with your choices?

I would like to go to a school to study medicine, in particular to become a naturopathic physician. I made sure that I chose schools that have a strong emphasis on the arts because I want the opportunity to continue with art and still have the option of pursuing it.

My foundation has made me want to continue with some form of art. Although I'm not sure what I want to do with my future, I know that I want there to be an artistic aspect to whatever I decide to do.

Without the art and writing support I got in middle school, I wouldn't have been so into writing and visual art. Because of that interest I continued to experiment with visual art, and discovered film and writing as very good creative outlets for me.

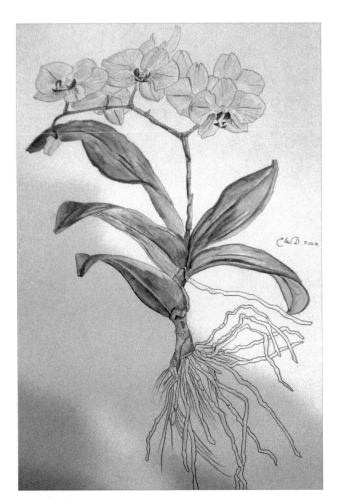

Will art continue to be part of your life? If so, how?

I am always working on projects and always will be. I make and sell fairy houses, jewelry and other things. I love making gifts and cards for people. I will always and forever be someone immersed in the arts.

I think it will definitely continue to be a big part of my life; however I'm not sure yet in which way.

Yes, I plan to always write whether I get a minor in it or not. I love to write and create stories. I am majoring in film production, and will continue to express my art through film.

Conclusions

The survey responses clearly indicate that drawing in the classroom in the elementary school years is meaningful and important. For many children learning how to write is a challenging task—drawing offers a relief from the potential strain of intellectual activity, or of merely the act of writing words onto the page.

Drawing enhances the child's experience at school and can foster a greater understanding of the material covered. Equally important is the act of drawing on its own, and the sensitivities that accompany it. Students can be crushed by comments from their peers and become reluctant to either continue or show their work to others.

The right guidance in the classroom can help steer things in a positive direction and make it a safe environment for students to work to their best potential. They can learn to take positive criticism and work with it to further improve their skills. They can also learn to give helpful criticism to others.

So much of the student's experience of art beyond elementary school is in the classroom within group settings and among peers. A basic foundation in the arts can foster the confidence necessary for the student to be able to function in high school in a way that is beneficial and conducive to personal growth in high school and beyond. Confidence in drawing can enhance a person's life beyond the classroom and serve to open the door to future enjoyment full of meaningful artistic activity.

Acknowledgments

I keep drawing the trees, the rocks, the river;
I'm still learning how to see them.
I'm still discovering their forms. I will spend a lifetime doing that.
Maybe someday I will get it right.

– Alan Lee

This book is dedicated to the wonderful Class of 2011 at Pine Hill Waldorf School in New Hampshire. Many thanks for the use of their artwork and quotes and for sharing their experiences over the eight years of drawing in the classroom. The journey we took together through the years was immeasurably enriched by the daily drawing experience and all the art projects we worked on together.

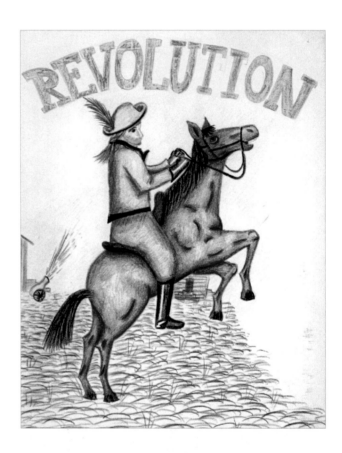

I want to express my special thanks to:

- Arthur Auer for his article on form drawing and for advice and inspiration, as well as technical support. He is the author of *Learning about the World through Modeling: Sculptural Ideas for the School and Home* and *Pure Form Modeling*.

- Van James for his insights on middle school arts and his contributions to the evolution of this book. He is the author of *Drawing with Hand, Head and Heart*. Van teaches at the Honolulu Waldorf School in Hawaii.

- Mary Graham, Nancy Crowe, David Kennedy and Amy Hilbert. Over the years of the book's evolution there are many to thank for their advice and support with editing and proofreading.

- Helen-Ann Ireland for contributing her article on the significance of daily drawing from her research on educational practices.

- Former teacher training students who gave permission to use their quotes, and for their most valuable feedback. Several of their blackboard drawings and quotes are sprinkled throughout the book. May they serve as inspiration for teachers to come.

- Thomas Buchanan, Elise Drapeau, Lily Hobbs, Emil Schroettnig and Steven Upton. The artwork from the first high school years included in the chapter on "Reflections" is testimony to the skills they gained during their elementary school years. May their artwork continue to flourish and enhance their learning about the world.

Bibliography

Reference books

Baravalle, Hermann von. *Perspective Drawing*. Fair Oaks, CA: Rudolf Steiner College Press, 1905.

Berry, L.H. (1991). "Visual complexity and the pictorial memory: A fifteen year research perspective." Paper presented at the annual meeting of the Association for Educational Communications and Technology. (ERIC Document Reproduction Service No. ED 334947), 1991.

Clausen, Anke and Martin Riedel. *Schöpferisches Gestalten mit Farben* [Creative Painting with Colors]. Stuttgart: Mellinger Verlag, 1972.

_____. *Zeichnen Sehen Lernen!* [Drawing and Learning to See]. Stuttgart: Mellinger Verlag, 1986.

Coles, Robert. *Their Eyes Meeting the World*. Boston: Houghton Mifflin Company, 1992.

Colquhoun, Margaret and Axel Ewald. *New Eyes for Plants*. Stroud, UK: Hawthorne Press, 1996.

Edwards, Betty. *Drawing on the Right Side of the Brain*. Boston: Houghton Mifflin Company, 1979.

Eisner, E.W. *The Arts and the Creation of the Mind*. New Haven: Yale University, 2002.

Franck, Frederick. *The Zen of Seeing*. New York: Vintage Books, Random House, 1973.

Gardner, H. *The Unschooled Mind: How Children Think and How Schools Should Teach*. New York: BasicBooks, 1991.

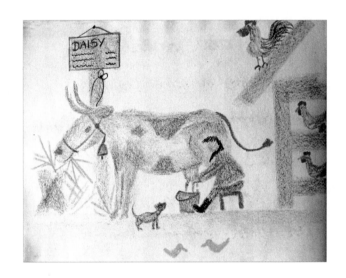

Gazzaniga, M. Dana Consortium report on arts and cognition, "Learning, arts, and the brain." New York/Washington DC: Dana Press, 2008.

Goleman, D. "The a-ha moment." http://www.youtube.com/embed/fZmTY8d9Jy4?autoplay=1&hd=1, 2011.

Hamm, Jack. *Drawing the Head and Figure*. London: Studio Books, 1963.

_____. *How to Draw Animals*. New York: Dover Publications, 1979.

Hetland, L., et al. *Studio Thinking: The Real Benefits of Visual Arts in Education*. New York and London: Teacher's College Press, 2007.

James, Van. *Drawing with Hand, Head and Heart*. Herndon, VA: SteinerBooks, 2013.

Jensen, E. *Arts with the Brain in Mind*. Alexandria, VA: ASCD, 2001.

Jünemann, Margrit and Fritz Weitmann. *Drawing and Painting in Rudolf Steiner Schools*. Stroud, UK: Hawthorne Press, 1976.

_____. *Blackboard Drawing*. Stuttgart: Verlag Freies Geistesleben, 1995.

Kellogg, Rhoda. *Analyzing Children's Art*. California: Mayfield Publishing Company, 1969.

Klocek, Dennis. *Drawing from the Book of Nature*. Fair Oaks, CA: Rudolf Steiner College Press, 1990.

Knapp, G.A.M. *Darkness and Light*. UK: Kolisko Archive Publication, 1982.

Langer, E.J. *Mindfulness*. Reading, MA: Addison-Wesley Pub. Co., 1989.

Lissau, Magda. *Temperaments and the Arts*. Fair Oaks, CA: AWSNA Publications, 2003.

Lowenfeld, Viktor and W. Lambert Britain. *Creative and Mental Growth*. New York: MacMillan Co., 1964.

McAllen, Audrey. *The Extra Lesson*. Stourbridge, UK: Robinswood Press, 1974.

_____. *Reading Children's Drawings*. Fair Oaks, CA: Rudolf Steiner College Press, 2004.

Malchiodi, Cathy. *Understanding Children's Drawings*. New York: Guilford Press, 1998.

Martin, Michael. *Light and Dark*. Switzerland: Verlag am Goetheanum, 1993.

Nicolaïdes, Kimon. *The Natural Way to Draw*. New York: Houghton Mifflin Company, 1941.

Pink, D.H. *A Whole New Mind: Why Right-brainers Will Rule the Future*. New York: Riverhead Books, 2006.

Schön, D.A. *The Reflective Practitioner: How Professionals Think in Action*. New York: BasicBooks, 1983.

Sobel, David. *Mapmaking with Children: Sense of Place Education for the Elementary Years* Portsmouth, UK: Heinemann, 1998.

Strauss, Michaela. *Understanding Children's Drawings*. London: Rudolf Steiner Press, 1988.

Turgeniev, Assya. *Reminiscences of Rudolf Steiner: Work on the First Goetheanum*. UK: Temple Lodge, 2003.

Walker, Leslie Clare. *Nature Drawing*. New York: Prentice Hall Press, 1980.

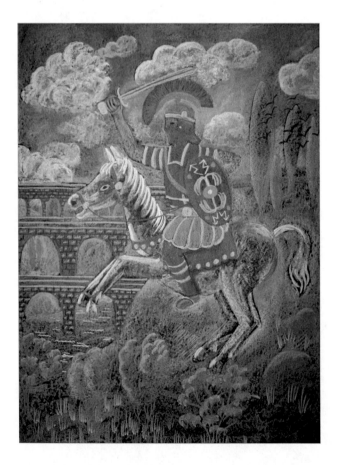

Form drawing bibliography

Numbers 1-6 are manuals for teachers:

1. Embrey-Stine, Laura and Ernst Schuberth. *Form Drawing: Grades One through Four*. Sacramento, CA: Rudolf Steiner College Press, 1999. An essential text for class teachers

2. Niederhauser, Hans and Margaret Frohlich. *Form Drawing*. Spring Valley, NY: Mercury Press, 1974. An essential text for class teachers

3. Kutzli, Rudolf. *Form Drawing: Workbooks I, II, III.* UK: Hawthorne Press, 1985. Inspiration for adults to enjoy form drawing and ideas for teachers

4. Hermann Kirchner. *Dynamic Drawing: Its Therapeutic Aspect.* Spring Valley, NY: Mercury Press, 1977. Many examples for the classroom

5. Kranich, Ernst and Margrit Jünemann. *Formenzeichnen* [Form Drawing]. Stuttgart: Verlag Freies Geistesleben, 1985. In German, but loaded with dozens of understandable form illustrations

6. Clausen, Anke and Martin Riedel. *Zeichnen Sehen Lernen!* [Drawing and Learning to See]. Stuttgart: Mellinger Verlag, 1986. In German, loaded with dozens of understandable form illustrations, including ones for introducing cursive writing

Bain, George. *Celtic Art: The Methods of Construction.* New York: Dover Publications, 1973.

Fein, Sylvia. *First Drawings: Genesis of Visual Thinking.* Martinez, CA: Exelrod Press, 1993.

Flinders Petrie, William. *Decorative Patterns of the Ancient World for Craftsmen.* New York: Dover Publications, 1974.

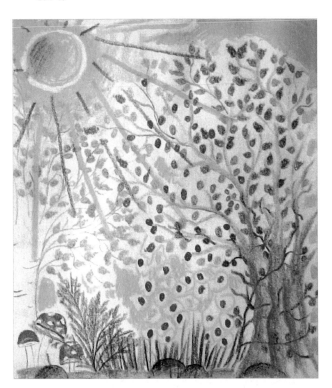

References to form drawing by Rudolf Steiner

Practical Advice to Teachers (Rudolf Steiner Press, 1976)
Lecture I (date 8-21-19)
p.18- archetypal forms-circle-spiral IV(8-24-19)
pp.59-60- important first lesson-straight/curved

Discussions with Teachers (1977) (temperaments) Lecture III (8-24-19)
p.41- for sanguine: melancholic
p.42- for choleric: cross enclosed in circle or curved star to pinwheel in circle
pp.42-43- for phlegmatic: opposite IV (8-25-19)
p.52- for sanguine-bumpy waves
p.52- for melancholic-fourfold petal-inner/outer colors

Faculty Meetings with Teachers (1988) (6-14-20)
p.98- spirals
p.99- circles-semicircles-triangles with feet (4-28-22)
p.332- remedial-circle-semicircle-completion-symmetry

Second Lecture on the Curriculum
p.199- rounded or angular forms-circles-ellipses-angles

Soul Economy XIV (1986) (1-5-22)
pp.251-252a- leaf-like r/l symmetry

A Modern Art of Education (1972) IX (8-14-23)
p.154- body of formative forces continues to vibrate, perfect, elaborate, calculate
p.155- head-like symmetry
p.155- three-petalled #1-transformation-correspondence inner and outer
p.156- three-petalled #2-correspondence inner-outer
p.157- alternative to intellectual triangles

The Kingdom of Childhood IV (8-15-24)
p.67- completing r/l symmetry
p.68- fourfold-transformation inner/outer transformations
p.69- reflection symmetry up/down

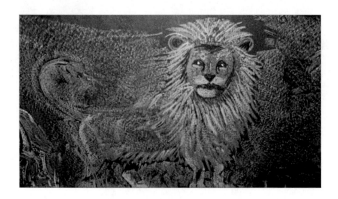

Other great books from the Waldorf-teaching Auer family

Learning about the World through Modeling: Sculptural Ideas for School and Home
by Arthur F. Auer, MEd
With over 175 exercises and illustrations
Available from Waldorf Publications

Creative Pathways: Activities that Strengthen the Child's Cognitive Forces
by Elizabeth Auer, MEd
Projects for the classroom grades 1-8
With over 100 illustrations and companion CD
Available from Waldorf Publications

Pure Form Modeling: Expanded Intelligence by Exploring Universal Shapes
by Arthur F. Auer, MEd
Illustrated with photos and drawings
14 series of modeling exercises and more
To be published soon

Wilson, Frank R. *The Hand: How It Shapes the Brain, Language and Culture*. New York: Pantheon Books, 1998.

_____. "The Real Meaning of Hands-on Education." *Research Bulletin*, January 2000, Research Institute for Waldorf Education, V (1), 2-14.

Howard, Michael. "Educating the Will: Part II: Developing Feeling Will in Contrast to Sense/Nerve Will." *Research Bulletin*, June 2002, Research Institute for Waldorf Education, VII (2), 16-23.

Further books of interest

Hale, Robert Beverly. *Drawing Lessons from the Great Masters*. New York: Watson Guptill Publications, 1964.

Mendelowitz, Daniel M., Duane A. Wakeham and David L. Faber. *A Guide to Drawing*, sixth edition. Thomson Wadsworth.

Norton, Dora Miriam. *Freehand Perspective and Sketching*. New York: Dover Publications, 2006.

Petherbridge, Deanna. *The Primacy of Drawing*. New York: Yale University Press, 2010.

Rayes, John. *The Complete Guide to Perspective*. UK: Collins and Brown, 2005.

Rosenberg, Pierre. *From Drawing to Painting*. Princeton University Press, 1996.

Ruskin, John. *Elements of Drawing*. London: Herbert Press Ltd., 1991.

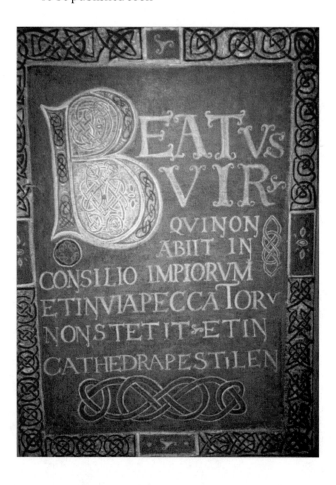

Made in the USA
Middletown, DE
18 August 2015